The Ultimate GIMP 2.10 Guide

Learn Professional photo editing

**This book accompanies 'The Ultimate GIMP 2.10 Guide'
video course on: Youtube.com/c/GraphicdesignforFree**

The Ultimate GIMP 2.10 Guide. Learn Professional photo editing.
By Bernard 't Hooft

ISBN: 978-1790584215

Printing History:

December 2018:	First Edition
June 2019:	Second Edition

CONTENTS

Chapter 1. Install & configure GIMP 2.10

Chapter 2. Working with Layers and color

Chapter 3. Making selections

Chapter 4. Cropping, Resizing, and more

Chapter 5. Google plugins

Chapter 6. Retouching

Chapter 7. Making e-book covers

Chapter 8. Adjusting Gimp's User Interface

Chapter 9. Gimp specifics

INDEX

Chapter 1

Install & configure GIMP 2.10

1. Introduction (please read before you start)

This book is the printed version of the free video course: *The Ultimate GIMP 2.10 Guide* on: **www.youtube.com/c/GraphicdesignforFree**.
With a printed version of the course, you get the best of both worlds!
If you have a question, you can send it to: **ultimategimpguide@gmail.com**.
I will answer within 48 hours!
The book has been printed in black and white to keep the price as low as possible. Although black and white doesn't compromise the learning experience, you will also get a Full Color PDF of the book, together with all the course resources, via a download link on YouTube.

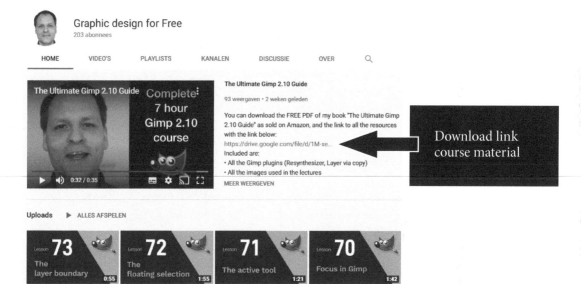

On my channel, to get to the lectures playlist, click on: 'playlists' (see image at the right). You will now see 'The Ultimate GIMP 2.10 Guide' playlist (whith 74 lectures). Click on the playlist image to start.
You can ask me questions in the comment section (visible for all students), but as a book owner, you are also able to e-mail me personally at:
ultimategimpguide@gmail.com

Good luck, and if you have any questions, please let me know!

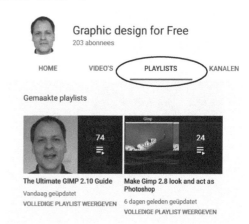

2. Installing Gimp

To download the latest version of Gimp, go to: *www.gimp.org*. At the moment of writing the latest version is 2.10.6. Click on the download button (1). The site thinks I am running Microsoft Windows (2), which is correct. Below I read that the installer contains both a

32-bit and a 64-bit version of GIMP, and that the appropriate version will automatically be installed. This means, that if your computer is a bit older, you can still use Gimp. I will click on the orange download button; Download Gimp directly (3). The download is about 175 MB.
Go to your Downloads folder and install Gimp (4).

Gimp can be found under the *'G'* in the Apps (5). Click on it to open Gimp.
The first time you start up Gimp, it takes a bit longer.
GIMP 2.10 will open as a single window, but if you're seeing separate floating windows, go to: *Windows >*, and choose: *Single-Window Mode* (6).

To attach the Gimp program thumbnail to your taskbar at the bottom for quick access, right-click on the Gimp thumbnail, and choose: *'Pin this program to taskbar'* (7).
To close Gimp you can go to: *File > Quit*, or you can click on the red close button at the upper right corner. To open Gimp again, you can now click on the thumbnail in the taskbar.

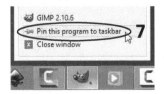

Gimp has a Fullscreen mode, which will hide the white bar at the top, and so provides more room in the height for your images. Go to: *View > Fullscreen*, or press *Shift-F* to enter Fullscreen mode (8). Press *Shift-F* again to leave Fullscreen mode.

In the next lecture we will install some plugins, to expand the functionality for Gimp.

3. Installing plugins

In this lecture we will install some files and plugins to expand the functionality of Gimp, and make Gimp work as Photoshop. The instructions are the same for everyone, whether you install plugins for the first time, or if you already have installed plugins, for example with the Ultimate Gimp 2.8 guide.

To expand the functionality of Gimp, we will install several files. Some of the files are the Resynthesizer and Layer-via-copy plugins. With **Resynthesizer**, known in Photoshop as *'Content aware filling'*, you can let Gimp remove objects for you (1). And **Layer-via-copy** is a great time-saver (2). With this plugin you need several steps less to place selected content on a new layer, and it makes the process identical to how it works in Photoshop. So the plugins provide added functionality and a faster workflow.

Together with the plugins we will also add some files that make Gimp look and act as Photoshop, Photoshop shortcuts included. And in Chapter 8 we will look at how to customize Gimp's User Interface to your personal likings.

The files that we will add can be downloaded from *Udemy.com*, as a downloadable zip file. At the right of the video player, you will see the videos (grouped in sections). Open *Section 1*, by clicking on it (3). When a video comes with downloadable material, a folder will also be visible. Click on the folder of lecture 3 (4). You will now see: *'Udemy.zip'*. If you click on *'Udemy.zip'*, the zip file will download automatically to your downloads folder. You can Unzip the file, or just double-click on it, to get to the content.

In the *'Udemy.zip'* folder you'll find (5):
- a **plug-ins folder** with *Resynthesizer* plugins, and the *Layer-via-copy* plugin,
- a **tool-options folder** that will make the *tools* in Gimp behave like they do in Photoshop,
- and **six additional files** that will make Gimp work as Photoshop.

Important: before you place these files, Gimp first has to be closed!

After you closed Gimp, you can now place the files from the *'Udemy.zip'* folder in a specific Gimp folder, where Gimp can see these files.

Because this specific Gimp folder is in a 'hidden' folder on your computer, we'll take a shortcut to reach the folder. Open the *File Explorer*. At the top

there are two windows. In the left window you see: *'This PC'* (6), and in the right window you see: *'Search This PC'* (7). We will use the *left* window. Click in the left window. The text *'This PC'* will become blue (8).

Now type (9):
`%appdata%`
So the *percent sign* (on my keyboard I can type it by pressing *Shift 5*), then *appdata*, and close off with the the *percent sign* again.

After having typed `%appdata%` press Enter. You will be brought to the following location:
This PC > your *'C' drive* > *Users* > then comes the name of your *'Home directory'* folder, which is in my case *'BernardPC'* > *AppData* > and *Roaming*. The *'AppData'* folder is the folder that is hidden in your *Home directory*.

In the *'Roaming'* folder we see the Gimp folder (10). Double-click on the Gimp folder. Now we see a folder called *'2.10'* (11), which is the folder we are looking for.
In Gimp 2.8 there was also such a folder, but it was placed directly in your *Home directory*, so the folder has moved to a new location.

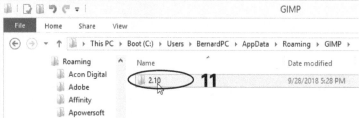

The *2.10* folder is the folder in which we're going to place the files, that we downloaded from Udemy. Before we do

this, we're going to make a copy of this folder, so we have a *back-up*. Right-click on the folder, and choose: *'Copy'*. Then right-click *below* the 2.10 folder, and choose: *'Paste'*. A *'2.10 - Copy'* folder is added, which is the back-up (12).

Now we'll change the content of the *2.10* folder. Double-click on the *2.10* folder to open it. Also open the *Udemy* folder. To select the content of the *Udemy* folder press *Ctrl-A*. Now all files and folders will be blue (13).

To copy the selected files and folders, press *Ctrl-C*. Click on the top of the *2.10* folder window (14), and press *Ctrl-V* to paste the files in the *2.10* folder. Now click on the text: *'Replace the files in the destination'* that is displayed in blue (15). After this, in the *2.10* folder, you will see the eight files and folders highlighted in blue, that you have copied over from the *Udemy* folder (16).

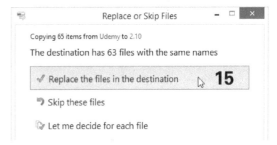

If you had additional plugins installed in the past, you can copy them over from the *'2.10 - Copy'* folder to the *2.10* folder (12).

Were now finished adjusting Gimp. In the next lecture, we'll explore Gimp's User Interface.

4. Exploring Gimp's User Interface

In this lecture, we'll explore Gimp's user interface. When you open Gimp after installing the plugins, you will see your user interface looks the same as mine. This will make following the course easy.

In Chapter 8, I will show you all the ways you can customize Gimp's user interface, so you can make it how you want it to look and act.

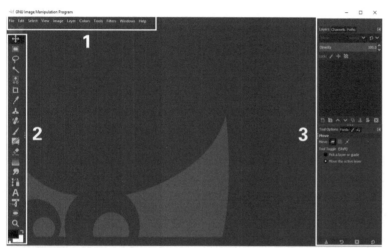

The user interface as we now have it, consists of a *menu bar* at the top (1), a *toolbar* at the left (2), and several *panels* at the right (3).

Now we make the program fit your screen. To do this, click at the top right on the *Maximize* icon (4).

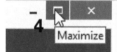

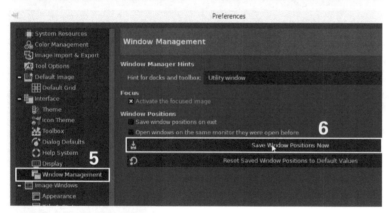

To save this UI change, go to: *Edit > Preferences*. In the Preferences panel click on the *Window Management* tab (5). Then click on: '*Save Window Positions Now*' (6).

To create a new document, go to: *File > New*. At the right side of the menu, we see you can also press '*Ctrl-N*' to create a new file (7). Click on *OK*.

At the right side, we have the *Tool Options* panel. The *Tool Options* panel will show you options you can choose from, and those options will be related to the tool you have selected at the left. When you open Gimp, by default the *Move tool* is selected (9). The *Move tool* is discussed in Lecture 6. If you want to use another tool, for example the *Paintbrush tool*, you can click on it, or can you press the letter *B*, which is indicated at the end of the tool description

(10). The *Tool Options* will now show different options, that are related to the *Paintbrush tool*. In Gimp 2.10 we now have a *Hardness* slider for the brush. Dragging the *Hardness* slider to the left will give a soft brush, and dragging it to the right will give a hard brush (11).

For some actions you can also use shortcuts. For example, to quickly adjust the size of the brush, like in Photoshop, you can press the *right bracket* key, to increase the size, and press the *left bracket* key, to decrease the size, when you're drawing on the canvas.

In lectures 9 and 10, the *Paintbrush* will be discussed in detail.

In Gimp 2.10, you can place and change shortcuts directly in the menus. Let's add a shortcut. To show how it works, I have left one shortcut out, which we will add it now. Go to: *View > Zoom > Fit Image in Window*. The keyboard shortcut for this command is *Control 0*. I place my mouse above the text, so that the text is highlighted (12). Then I press the *Control* key together with the *0* key (13). I will use the numeric 0 (zero) key for this, which is at the bottom right of my keyboard. If you don't have an extra numeric 0 key on your keyboard, you can use the 0 key above the characters.

How to zoom and pan in Gimp is further discussed in lecture 8.

In the next lecture, we will look at opening images in Gimp.

Chapter 2
Working with layers and color

5. Opening files

To open an image, go to *File > Open*. Notice you can find it's shortcut, *Ctrl-O*, at the right side of the command. If you click on Open, the *Open Image* window opens.

At the left side, under *Places* (1), is the navigation pane. From here you can access your desktop, your home directory, the drives on your PC, etc. I will navigate to a folder on my desktop called *Gimp*. At the left I click on *Desktop*. Then I double-click on the *Gimp* folder to see its content. At the top you can see the folders path: *BernardPC > Desktop > Gimp* (2). To exit the Gimp folder again, and go one step back, at the top, I can click on the *Desktop* thumbnail, at the left of the *Gimp* thumbnail (2).

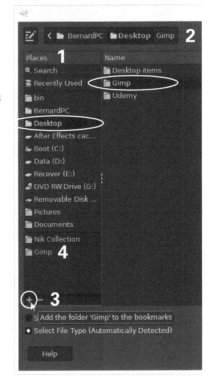

If you visit a specific folder often, you can *bookmark* that folder for quick access. To bookmark a folder first click on a folder. At the bottom left you will see a *plus sign* (3). When you click on the plus sign, the selected folder is added to *Places*, at the bottom (4). To remove a bookmarked folder from the list, click on the bookmark. At the right of the plus sign is a *minus sign*. Click on the minus sign to remove a bookmark.

To see a preview of an image you click on the image name. You can also use your up and down arrow keys to browse through a list of images.

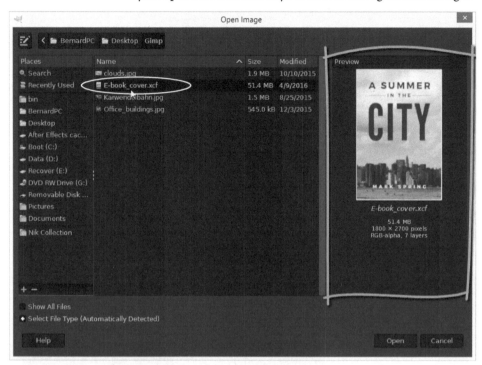

By default, the content of a folder is sorted on alphabetical order (*Name*). But you can also sort on date (*Modified*), or sort on file size (*Size*). To *reverse* a column; to turn it around (for example *file Size*) click on the *Size* thumbnail. Now the list starts with the *smallest* file size, and ends with the *largest* file size (5).

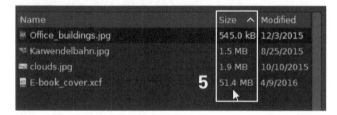

I click on *Office_buildings.jpg* and click on Open.

In the next lesson we will look at how to work with layers.

6. Working with layers

As a child, I was fascinated by the way the old Walt Disney cartoons were made. Walt Disney broke down a scene in *moving* and *non-moving* parts. He painted them on different transparent sheets, and laid these transparent sheets on top of each other. Working this way, *only* the sheets with the *changing* elements had to be repainted.

Walt Disney's way of working isn't that different from how we work in Gimp and Photoshop today. Let's open an image with Walt Disney's way of working in mind. Open *Cartoon.xcf*. The images used here come from *Freepik.com*. Open *Layers* by clicking on the *Layers* tab (1). We can see the scene is broken up in three transparent sheets, which in their digital form are now called *layers*.

On the bottom layer is the image of the background. Above the background, we have a layer with only the air balloon on it. And on top we have a layer with only the girl on it.

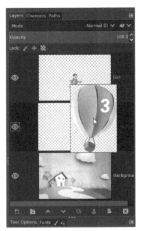

I have made the layer *thumbnails* a bit larger, so you can better see their content. To do this, click at the right on the *Configure this tab* icon (2), then go to *Preview Size*, and choose *Gigantic*.
Now you can clearly see what is on the three layers. If you hold your mouse pressed down on a layer thumbnail, you get an even bigger preview of its content, as we can see with the air balloon (3).

You can move the layers *independent* of each other. To move the girl layer, select the layer where the girl is on, by clicking on that layer. Also select the *Move* tool. The *Move* tool can be found in the toolbar at the left (4). You can click on it, or press the letter *V* to select it. Now you can move the girl around by dragging on the canvas (5).

If you press *Ctrl-Z*, which can be found under: *Edit > Undo*, you undo your move, and the girl is back where you started. And if you want to move the air balloon, click on the air balloon layer, and move the air balloon.

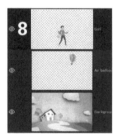

With the air balloon layer selected, you can't move the girl. However, if you click in the *Tool Options* on: *Pick a layer or guide* (6), it will become possible. If you now place your mouse *above* the girl, you will see a *hand* appearing at the right side of the cursor (7). Even though the girl layer is *not* the selected layer, you *are* able to move her now. After moving the girl layer, the girl layer will now *also* be the *selected* layer, as it is in Photoshop (8).

This way of moving we just did, *isn't* set as the default in Gimp, and also isn't the default in Photoshop. The reason for this is the possibility of moving other layers *by accident*, without noticing. However, when you quickly have to move several different layers, it's possible to do this quickly by selecting the *Pick a layer* option. I will select the *Move the active layer* option again.

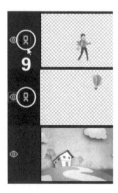

It's also possible to move more than one layer at the same time. Let's say you want to drag the girl layer *together* with the air balloon layer. To do this you can temporarily *link* these layers. If you click between the eye and the thumbnail, a *chain icon* appears (9). Layers that have a chain, are linked to each other. If you move a layer that has a chain, other layers that also have a chain, will move with it. To remove a chain, click on the chain again.

The *checkerboard* pattern is a visual way to show empty space. It's like the transparent sheet from the old days; where there was no paint, you could look *through* it. Our background is completely filled. However, if we move the background to the side, we also get to see the checkerboard pattern.

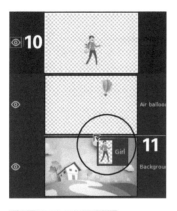

To change the *stacking order* of a layer, simply drag the layer up or down. Right now, the girl is *in front* of the air balloon (10). If I want to place her *behind* the air balloon, I drag the girl layer down.

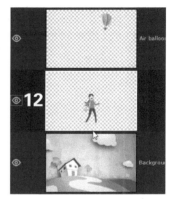

When you see an extra arrow and a white line appearing (11), release the mouse. The girl is now behind the air balloon (12, 13).

You can also click on the up and down *arrows* to move a layer up or down (14). I will put her back on top.

You can hide a layer by clicking on the eye at the left of the layer thumbnail. Click there again, and the layer is visible again. If you *Shift*-click on a layers eye, you will *solo* that layer. This means you will see *only* that layer, and hide all other layers (15). *Shift*-click on the eye again, and all layers are visible again.

You can also lower a layer's *Opacity*. Lowering a layer's Opacity means you make the content on that layer more *transparent*. This means you can then look *through* the content.

Select the girl layer. When you place your cursor in the opacity bar (16), you will see an arrow that points upwards. If you drag to the left, you will slowly see the girl disappear (17, 18).

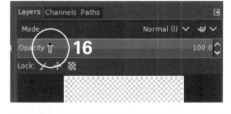

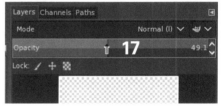

When you *right-click*, the arrow will change to a *double-sided* arrow (19). The double-sided arrow can be used for fine-tuning. And when your cursor is *inside* the Opacity bar, you can also use your *scroll wheel* to adjust the opacity. Holding down the *Ctrl* key while scrolling will make the value change in *larger steps*.

When you know the exact percentage you want, you can directly *type* it, by *double-clicking* on the text at the right, type a number, and press Enter.

If you want to *delete* a layer you click on it, and at the bottom right click on the little *cross*. You can undo this by pressing *Ctrl-Z*.

You can make a *duplicate* of a layer by clicking on the *Create a duplicate* button (20). Let's duplicate the girl. Now we have two layers with the girl on it. I drag it to the side (21). I delete the duplicate again.

You can create a *new* and empty layer, by holding the *Shift* key down, and then click on the *Create a new layer* button (22). If you get a layer that is not empty, click on the *Create a new layer* button without the Shift key, and behind *Fill with*, choose: *Transparency* (23), and click on OK. From now on when you *Shift*-click on the *Create a new layer* button, you will get an empty layer.

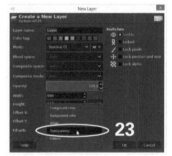

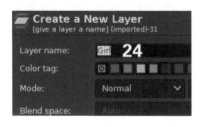

You can give a layer a *name*. The more layers you get, the more helpful this will be for quickly recognising what's on a layer. You can double-click on a layers *thumbnail*, type a name (24), and press Enter. You can also double-click on the *text itself* at the right side of the layers thumbnail, type a name, and press Enter.

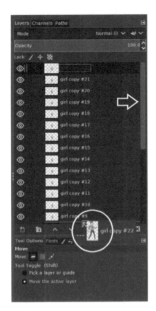

I have set the layer thumbnails to *medium* size again, and copied the girl layer several times to get more layers than the panel can show. I am now *still* able to *drag* a layer to another place. If I drag a layer from the top completely to the bottom, the panel will *auto scroll* (see the change of the scroll bar, between the left and right image).

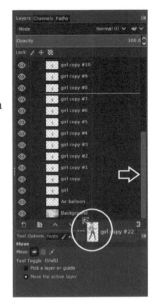

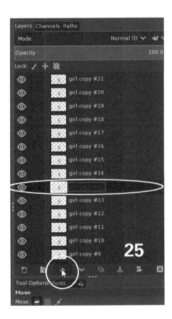

The fastest way to place a layer on *top* or on the *bottom*, is to *Shift*-click on the pointing *up* arrow to place the layer at the top (25, 26), or *Shift*-click on the pointing *down* arrow to place the layer at the bottom.

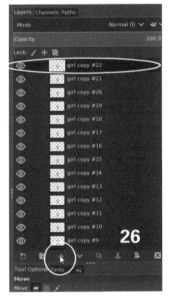

In the next lesson we will look at a special layer: the Background.

7. The 'background' layer

Gimp and Photoshop have a lot in common. One of these things is the mystery of the *Background* layer. So, what is the Background layer? If you create a *new* document, you will start with a special layer: the *Background*. In Photoshop you can recognize the Background because it has *italic* text instead of normal text. In Gimp you can recognize the Background because it has *bold* text instead of normal text.

The Background is different from a normal layer, because you can't look through it or behind it. This transparency is sometimes needed, for example when the image will be used as a logo on the internet, and you want to be able to see the web page *behind* the transparent parts of logo (see p. 112).
So how do we change this?

In both Photoshop and Gimp you can *right*-click on the Background.
In Photoshop you choose: *Layer from background* (1). In Gimp, you choose: *Add Alpha Channel* (2). Both do the same. In Gimp, the *bold* text will now change to *normal* text. The Background has become a normal layer.

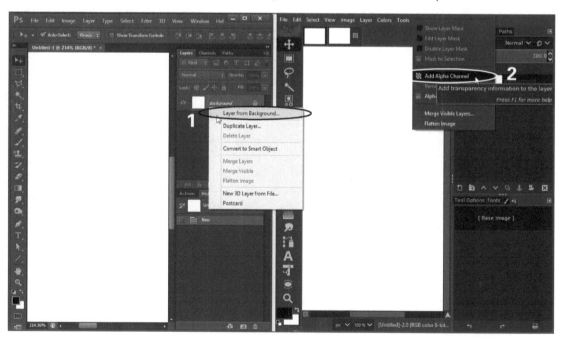

In the next lecture we will look at how to navigate in Gimp.

8. Zooming and panning

For this lesson, open *Mountains.jpg*. There are two main ways of navigation: zooming and panning. Let's start with zooming.

Zooming means zooming in and zooming out. The fastest way to zoom is by scrolling with the mouse wheel while holding down the *Ctrl* key. If you scroll forward, you zoom *in*, if you scroll backward, you zoom *out*. The place you hold your mouse, is the place you will zoom in on. This is very efficient. Let's say I want to zoom in on a screw. I hold my cursor above it (1), press *Ctrl*, and scroll forward (2). If you zoom in very far, you will start to see the building blocks of the image, the *pixels*.

Another way to zoom is using the *Zoom* tool. It's located at the bottom of the toolbar. With the Zoom tool you can drag an *exact area* you want to zoom in on (3).

The fastest way to zoom out again is by pressing: *Ctrl-0*. *Ctrl-0* will *fit* the image perfectly on the screen. Although fitting an image on the available space on screen is very useful, it *doesn't* mean that you then see the image at its *real* size. To see an image at it's *real* size, it's zoom percentage has to be: 100%. Anything *higher* than 100% means you're zoomed in, anything *lower* than 100% means you're zoomed out.

The zoom percentage is shown at the bottom of the screen. We see: *19,6 %* (4). This means we're zoomed *out*. The image is *much larger*, than what we see right now.

When you see an image at it's *real* size, so at 100%, *each* pixel of the *image*, will correspond to a pixel of your *screen* (so an *exact* match). The shortcut for real size, or 100%, is: *Ctrl-1*.

The second way of navigating is panning. When you're zoomed *in* on an image, you can move around, or pan, by pressing down your *scroll* wheel, and then move your mouse.

You can also just scroll with your mouse wheel to move up and down. And when you add the *Shift* key while scrolling, you will move to the left and the right.

For moving over *longer distances*, dragging the scroll bar at the right (5) and at the bottom works fast and efficient.

Finally, at the bottom right of the canvas there is the *Navigate display* (6). When you click on the little *arrow*, a thumbnail of the image appears (7).

In the *Navigate display* you can move around by dragging inside the *white border*. The white border represents the visual canvas.

In the next lesson we will explore the paintbrush.

9. Using the paintbrush

Now let's look at the paintbrush. Open *White Beach.jpg*. Before using the paintbrush, I will create a new empty layer, so I am not painting on the image, but on a separate layer (and so leave the image in tact).

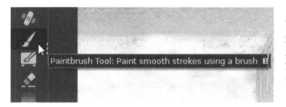

Click on the *Paintbrush* tool in the toolbar. You can also press: *B* to select the Paintbrush.

To change the *size* of the brush, press the *Alt* key, and scroll forward to increase the size (1), and scroll backward to decrease the size (2).

In the *Tool Options*, you can see the size of the brush changing. I set the size to 60. The color you'll will be painting with comes from the *Foreground* color, which is by default set to black (3). Behind the Foreground color is the *Background* color (4), which is by default set to white. You can turn them around by clicking on the little double arrow, or by pressing the *X* key.

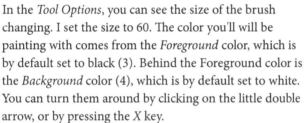

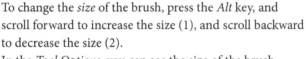

To draw a stroke you drag.

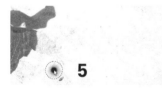

To draw a straight line, click once (5), then press *Shift*, and with Shift pressed down, click somewhere else (6).

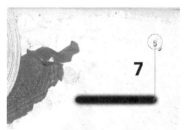

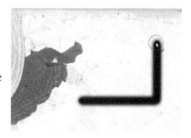

To get a straight *horizontal* or *vertical* line, press *Shift* plus *Control*. The thin line (7) is a *preview* to help you see where the stroke will be.

In the *Tool Options*, you can see a small thumbnail (8). This is the brush you're currently using. If you click on it, you will get an overview of all the brushes you have (9). I have added some additional brushes. At the end of lesson 11, I will show you where you can download *free* creative brushes.

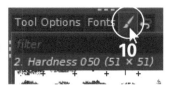

Another way to select a brush is by going to the *Brushes* panel (10). I open it. The advantage of the *Brushes* panel is that you can make the panel larger, by dragging at the left side.

As in the *Layers* panel, you can also make the *thumbnails* of the brushes bigger in the *Brushes* panel. I click on *Configure this tab*, go to *Preview size*, and I select *Extra large*.

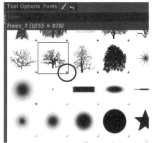

A small *plus* sign at the bottom right of a brush icon means that the *actual* brush size is *larger* than the preview size. As in the layers panel, you get a *larger* preview if you click on the thumbnail and hold the mouse button down (11).

A brush with a *red triangle* is called an *animated* brush. An animated brush will alternate different brushes while you paint, so it gives variation in the paint result.

This is a normal brush (12).

I delete the content of the layer by pressing the *Delete key*.

And this is an *animated* brush (13).

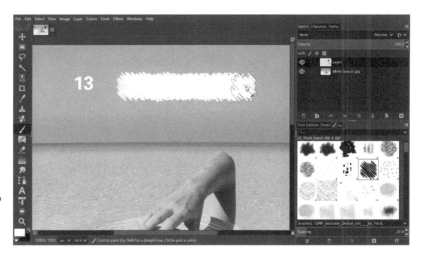

Now we will look at the relation between the *Opacity* slider and the *Force* slider of the brush. I select a hard round brush, and set the size to 100. I paint with black. Instead of lowering the Opacity of the *layer* I paint on, I can also lower the Opacity of the *brush*. I set it on 50%. If I now paint, the brush will be 50% opaque (14).

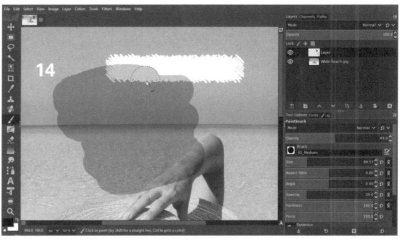

When you *release* the mouse button, and paint again, you'll add another 50% black (15). With Opacity being set lower, the brush won't get darker when you paint over and over the same area (holding down the mouse button). This is not a very natural way of adding paint. We are used that if we paint with a marker, repeatedly over an area, that area becomes darker. This is what the *Force* slider will do. *Force* provides the *natural* way of adding paint.

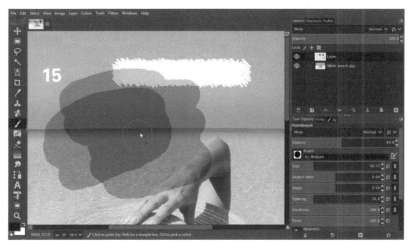

I set Opacity to 100%, and set *Force* to 20%. I set Hardness to 25%, and the size to 300. If I now paint over and over the same place (without releasing the mouse button), the black gradually builds up (16), until I get 100% black.

You can also *combine* Opacity and Force. Opacity will then become a limiter of the *maximum* black that the brush can reach. To prevent that the hat becomes completely black, I set Opacity to 80%. If I release the mouse, and paint over and over the same spot again, the hat will *still* not become completely black (although darker than before) (17).

In the next lecture we will look at special effects for brushes.

10. Brush special effects

In the Tool Options, if you click on the *icon* at the left of *Dynamics* (1), you will see a list with options (2). Select: *Velocity Tapering*. What *Velocity Tapering* does is, it decreases the *size* ánd *opacity* of your brush, when you move your mouse *faster* (3).

Below *Dynamics*, there is an option *Apply Jitter* (4). *Jitter* will spread the brush randomly (5). When you select *Apply Jitter*, you can set the *Amount*. Increasing *Amount* will lead to a *larger area* in which the spreading will take place. I set Jitter to about 4 by dragging in the Amount bar (6).

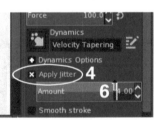

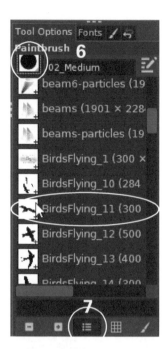

Click on the icon at the left of *Dynamics* again, and now select: *Speed Size Opacity*. To demonstrate this Dynamic, I will use a brush I have downloaded, named *Birdsflying_11*. At the end of the next lesson I will show you where you can download free brushes.

To search a brush *by name*, in the *Tool Options*, click on the brush thumbnail (6), and then select *View as list* at the bottom (6). To go through the list fast you can drag the scroll bar at the right. When you're close to the destination, you can further scroll with your scroll wheel. I select *Birdsflying_11*.

I choose black to paint black birds. I *Alt*-scroll to set the brush size to 150, and I will increase *Jitter* to 15.
We can see that *Speed Size Opacity* follows the *direction* of the *mouse* (8, 9 10). It also *decreases* the size of the brush when you move the mouse faster.

The next dynamic I would like to show you is *Dynamics random*. I will choose another downloaded brush, named *bubble_brushes_by_hawksmont3*.
I will set the size to 250, and press *X* to paint with white (11).

To show the next brush I will make a white layer. I create an empty layer by *Shift*-clicking on the *Create a new layer* button. To fill the layer with white, I

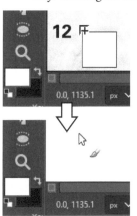

drag the Foreground color, which is white now, *on* the canvas (12). This way of filling is *Gimp only*. You can't do this in Photoshop. The Photoshop way of filling can be found under: *Edit > Fill with FG color*. The shortcut for this is *Alt-Backspace* (13).

I will turn the Fore- and Background colors around, by pressing the X key.

I will now set the Foreground color to red. I open the Color panel, and drag the Red slider to 80%.

We will make a grungy effect. In the *Tool Options* I select a brush called: *Acrylic 05*. Gimp's default brushes are at the bottom. I set the brush size to 400, and disable *Jitter*.

When I set *Dynamics* on *Perspective*, I can make grungy strokes.

14

To draw with chalk, I select *Texture Hose 01*. I set the brush to a 100% hard brush, size 20.

15
16

When I set Dynamics to *Fade Tapering* the brush will fade in or out. Right now it fades in (14).

When you open *Dynamics Options* (15), you can *reverse* the fading direction by clicking on *Reverse* (16). I will also increase the Fade length a bit (to 432), by dragging the slider.

17

Now the brush fades out (17).

Each time you start up Gimp, *Pressure Opacity* is the default brush Dynamic. For the mouse, *Pressure Opacity* has no effect. But if you are using a tablet, it enables you to draw with *pressure sensitivity*. In the next lesson we will look at using a tablet.

11. Using a tablet

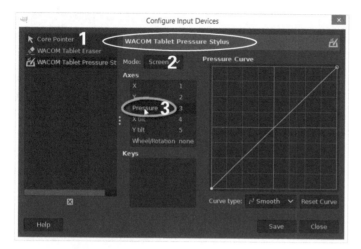

In this lesson we will look at the tablet preferences. Go to: *Edit > Preferences > Input Devices > Configure Extended Input Devices*. I have connected a *Wacom Tablet Pressure Stylus* as we can see at the top. The *Core Pointer* (1) is my mouse. Below we see: *WACOM Tablet Eraser*, which is the bottom of my pen, with which I can erase. The *Wacom Tablet Pressure Stylus* is the top of my pen, with which I can draw. Both are set on *Screen* (2).

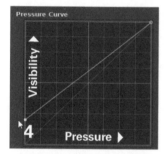

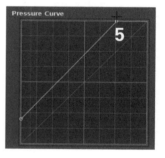

When I click on *Pressure* (3), I can change the *sensitivity* of the tablet. The horizontal axis, is pen *pressure*, starting with low pen pressure to higher pen pressure. The vertical axis is the *brush visibility*, starting from not visible, to fully visible. So the harder I press my pen, the darker or more visible the brush will become.

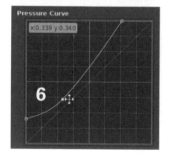

Let's say I want to press *less hard* before I start to see my brush. I can adjust this by dragging the *left side* of the graph up (4). And if I want to press less hard before I reach the *maximum* brush visibility, I drag the *right side* of the graph to the *left* (5).

For fine-tuning, I would like that pressing just a bit harder doesn't lead to high brush visibility so fast. To do this, I will flatten the graph at the beginning a bit by dragging it down (6). You will see an *extra point* is automatically created to make this possible.

To save the tablet settings, I click on *Save*, and then on *Close*.

If the *back* of the pen *doesn't* erase, you can do the following: select the *Erase Tool* (7) with the *back* of the pen, and then *use* the back of the pen (8).

To download *free* brushes, you can do a Google search for: *gimp free brushes*. There are several websites you can go to. I downloaded my brushes from *deviantart.com*. Click on the Browse tab, and in the Search box type: *gimp brushes*. If you scroll to the bottom you can click on *Show more*. If you find a brush-pack you like, you can click on it.

At the right, you will see a download button. After downloading, Unzip the file.

A *.gbr* extension stands for: *gimp brush*, and a *.gih* extension stands for: *gimp animated brush*. Go to the *2.10 folder* where you've placed the plugins, and open the *brushes* folder. Place the downloaded brushes in this folder. In Gimp, I go to the *Brushes* panel, and click at the bottom right on the *Refresh brushes* icon (9). The new brushes are now ready to use.

In the next lecture we will look at the MyPaint brush.

12. The Mypaint brush

The *MyPaint brush* (1) is a new brush in Gimp 2.10. To see what the *MyPaint brush* can do, we'll compare it with the normal *Paintbrush* (2). I will start with the Paintbrush, and then switch to the MyPaint Brush to see how they differ. I will create a new document by going to: File > New, and click OK.

I will click on the Foreground color and make a green color by dragging the green slider all the way to the right. Then I click on the Background color, click in the red square, and drag to the top right. This will give pure red. I click on OK. I select the *Paintbrush*. I set the size to 200, and paint on the canvas. Now I turn my colors around to paint with red. In the Tool options I lower *Force* to 10. When I paint over the green, there is no interaction between the colors, as paint would do (3). I press *Ctrl-Z* to remove the red strokes. Now I select the *MyPaint brush*. As I drag over the green, I see there is now real interaction between the red and green colors (4).

3

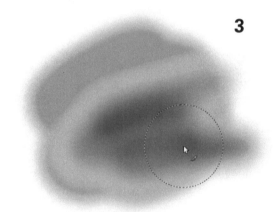

4

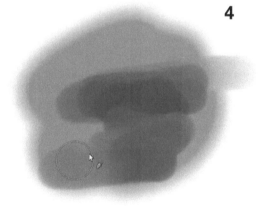

To choose another brush, click on the brush thumbnail (5). There are many MyPaint Brushes to choose from. I scroll down and select *paint sm*, which will let me smear paint (6).

So the MyPaint Brush offers new expressive art-brushes that respond to color in a more natural way. This is ideal for digital painting.

Digital painters can now *rotate* the canvas by pressing the *Shift key*, and then pressing the middle mouse button, which normally is the scroll wheel, down, and drag.

To reset the canvas, press *Shift-1*, or go to: *View > Flip and Rotate > Reset Flip and Rotate*.

In the next lesson we will look at how to back in time with the History panel.

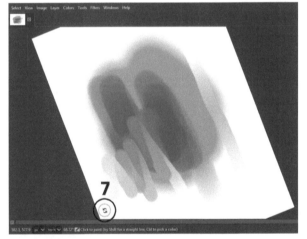

13. The history panel

For undoing multiple steps, in Gimp and Photoshop you have the *History* panel. To see how the *History* panel works, we'll create a new document. Go to: *File > New*. I make *Width* and *Height* 500 pixels.

If you open *Advanced Options*, you will see *Fill with* is by default the *Background color*. This means the new document will be filled with white. Click on OK.

Open the *History* panel at the bottom right. In the *History* panel we see: *Base Image*. Select the *Paintbrush* tool, and in the *Tool Options* select a hard brush. Set the size to 150. Open the *History* panel again.

When I click with my brush at the top left of my document to add a point, a new state is added to the *History* panel (1). The thumbnail visually shows us a point is added, and in the description we can read that we used the *paintbrush* to do this. Let's click three more times. I can now see I have used the *paintbrush* four times (2).

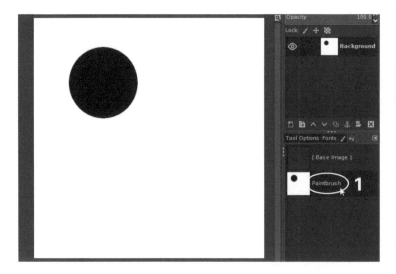

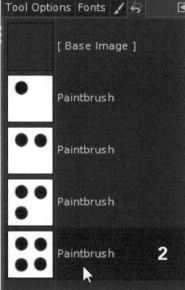

Let's say at this point I realize I made a mistake. I wanted 3 dots *diagonally*.

To go back in time, I can click on a previous state. I can also use my up- and down *arrow* keys, to 'walk' through my history. Nothing will be deleted when you navigate through your history.

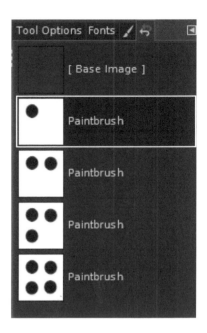

I would like to go back to the situation where I had just *one* point. I want this state to be my new starting point. When I start working from this point, a new state will be added again, but all the *future* states will be *deleted*. This deleting cannot be undone. If you want to prevent this deleting, continue working in a *duplicate* of your file. Go to: *Image > Duplicate*, to duplicate your file. The *duplicated* image has the state that was *selected* in your *original* file in the *History* panel, when you made the duplicate. You can now continue working in the *duplicated* file, while in the *original* image all the future states are still intact! At the moment you are sure that you *don't* need these future states anymore, you can delete the original file.

The number of steps you can go back in time is not infinite, however normally sufficient. If you're not satisfied with the amount of steps you can go back, you can go to: *Edit > Preferences*, or press *Ctrl-K*. The absolute minimum number of undo levels is now set to 5. This means Gimp guarantees, that you can go *at least* 5 steps back, at any time (3). The *actual* number of steps you can go back is normally much higher, dependent of how *large* your file is, and how *memory intensive* your changes were.

Maximum undo memory (4) is for computers that don't have much RAM.

If a computer hasn't much RAM, lowering the amount of allocated RAM for Maximum undo memory, *together* with lowering the *Minimal number of undo levels*, can help increasing overall performance. For computers that have a sufficient amount of RAM, *Maximum undo memory* does not have to be adjusted.

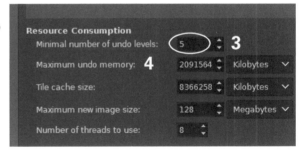

In the next lesson we will look at color.

14. HSV color

Image manipulation programs are all about color. How to select color, and how to change color. If we zoom in closely on an image, we see that an image consists of *squares*, with each square having its own color. These squares are called *pixels*, and a digital camera captures millions of them in a photo. One million pixels is often referred to as a megapixel.

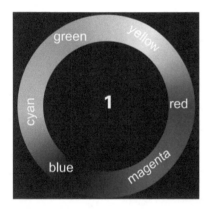

To get a better understanding of how you can manipulate color, we'll look in this lesson at the *three core components* that define color. They are described in the *HSV color model*, which is short for: *Hue*, *Saturation*, and *Value*. In Gimp and Photoshop you can adjust each of these color components *separately*, which is really powerful.

The first component of HSV is *Hue*, which can be *any color* on the Hue ring (1).
The second component is *Saturation*. The colors on the Hue ring are *fully* saturated.

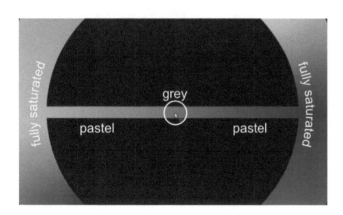

If we *connect* the colors from one side of the ring, to the opposite side of the ring, we will see that in the *middle* we find pure *grey*, which means colors in the middle have become fully *unsaturated*. So at the *edge* all colors are fully saturated, and in the *center* all colors have become fully *unsaturated*. When a color is going from fully saturated more to grey, we call it *pastel* colors. So colors in the center are fully unsaturated, than they go to *pastels*, and at the outside the colors are fully saturated.

The third and last component is *Value*. Value determines how *dark* or how *light* a color is. Bringing the Value down, which is the same as bringing in *black*, leads to darker, *shadowy* colors. Bringing the Value up, which is the same as bringing in *white*, makes the colors *lighter*. When colors become white, they are said to be *fully illuminated* (2).

To represent Hue, Saturation, and Value *all three together*, we would get a *cylindrical* model.

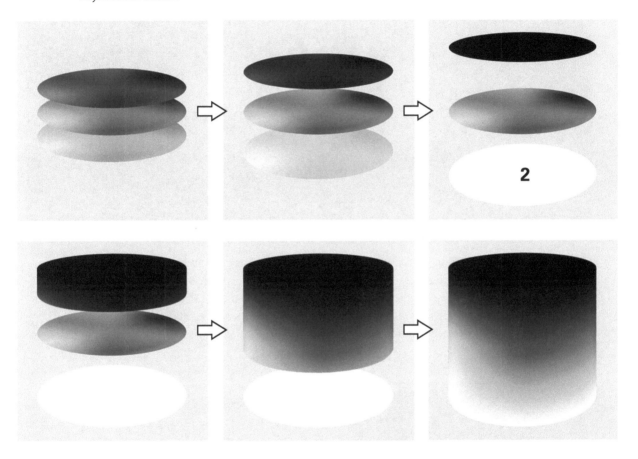

In the next lecture we will look at the RGB color model.

15. RGB color

In the previous lecture we have looked at Hue, Saturation, and Value, as described in the *HSV color model*. In this lecture we will look at the *RGB color model*. RGB stands for *Red*, *Green*, and *Blue*. It is the color model that a digital camera uses, as well as your computer screen. An image from a digital camera is actually built up from three images: a *red*, a *green*, and a *blue* image (1, 2, 3).

This means that *each pixel* of an image has information about how much red, green, and blue it contains. If we compare the red, green, and blue images, we can see that the sky in the *red* image is very dark (1). The sky in the *green* image is lighter (2), and the sky in the *blue* image is the lightest. We will see what this means in a moment.

Click on Foreground color, to open the *Change Foreground Color* window. At the top, we see the RGB color model, and when I click at the top right on HSV (4), we also get to see the HSV color model we have looked at in the previous lecture. With the three RGB sliders you're able to make the *same* colors as you can, with the three HSV sliders. So the RGB and HSV color models can be used together! This means, the RGB and HSV sliders can be used interchangeably, as we will see later. Right now we have the color black, which indicates that the Red, Green, and Blue (and HSV) sliders don't have any value (5). They're all at 0 percent.

With the sliders we can change this. Let's adjust the *red*, *green*, and *blue* values, and see what happens. I start by dragging the Red slider all the way to the right (6). We now get *full* red, and red has become a value of 100%.

Now let's also drag the Green slider all the way to the right. The result is that we see yellow! The color yellow is somewhat counterintuitive, because we are *used* to mixing paint on paper, and mixing red and green *doesn't* make yellow.

The answer lies in the terms *additive*, versus *subtractive* color. RGB is an *additive* color system. In this image we can see how it works. The image represents a fully *unilluminated* white wall, which is illuminated by three *colored* flashlights; a *red*, a *green*, and a *blue* flashlight. Where two flashlights *overlap*, the color changes, and the wall gets *brightened up* even more. In the middle, where the *red*, *green*, and *blue* flashlights *all* overlap, we are now able to see the wall as it is; in *white*! This is how the RGB color model works. The white wall is made visible by *adding* colored lights, hence the name *additive* color. When we *print* an image, all the paint will do, is make the *already* white and illuminated paper *darker*, hence the name *subtractive* color. So additive and subtractive color work in *opposite* ways.

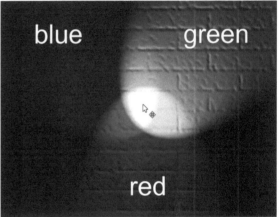

Where the red and green flashlights overlap, we get yellow.

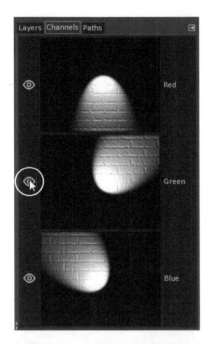

A digital camera works with the RGB color model. This means a digital camera will capture *three* images; a red, a green, and a blue image. Gimp and Photoshop will *show* us these three images, in the panel at the right side of Layers, called *Channels*. So the red, green, and blue images are called *channels*. Gimp shows each channels on the canvas in *color* for us, but the channels are actually just *black and white* images (as is shown in the thumbnails).

As you can hide layers, you can also hide channels. So hiding the Green channel, will turn the green flashlight off.

When we look at the channels of a Hue ring (a ring with all colors), we can see *all* Hues are created with only three basic colors. How is this possible?

The reason for this is that our eyes can *also* perceive *only* red, green, and blue information. Our brain does the rest; it will mix these three basic colors, and we see *all* colors.

To create a certain color in the *Change Foreground Color* window, you can also drag your mouse in the *color square* at the left. Here we see a *horizontal* line (7), and a *vertical* line (8).

The *vertical* line is the *Saturation* of a color. Dragging Saturation to the left will desaturate the color, dragging Saturation to the right will increase the saturation of the color.

The *horizontal* line is the *Value* of a color. Moving it *down* makes the color darker, moving it *up* makes the color lighter.

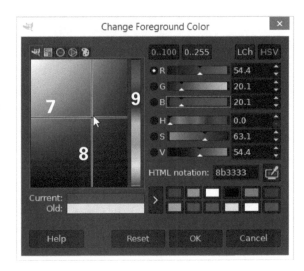

The *Hue* of a color can be chosen at the right side of the square (9); in the *hue strip*. The *hue strip* is a *straightened* Hue ring. You can slide through the hues by dragging (10).

You can add colors to the *Color history* by clicking on the arrow button at the left of the color swatches (11). The *Color history* consists of 12 color icons below the *HTML notation*. When a new color is added, all colors shift one place to the right, and the oldest swatch (at the bottom right) will be deleted.

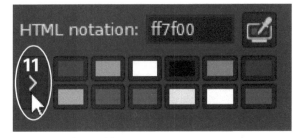

If you need the HTML, or *hexadecimal* notation of a color for the internet, you can copy it's value from above the color history.

In the next lecture we will look at how to make an image darker or lighter (*Value*), with Levels.

16. Levels

In the *HSV color model*, we saw the three basic elements of color are: *Hue*, *Saturation*, and *Value*. Levels is a powerful tool to adjust *Value*. So with Levels you can change how dark or light an image is.

Open *Amsterdam.jpg*. Here we have an image of Amsterdam, taken with a bright sky in the background. To protect the image from overexposure, the camera closed its lens a bit. As a result of this, the darker areas in the image didn't get enough light. Fortunately, in an image manipulation program it's easy to correct for underexposure.

Open Levels by going to: *Colors > Levels*, or press *Ctrl-L*. In the window there are five sliders. For *most* corrections, however, you will be using only *one*; the *middle* slider at the top (1). This slider is very powerful. With this slider you're able to make your image darker or lighter, *without* losing the darkest or lightest colors. This means the *Value* of all colors are intelligently *stretched*.

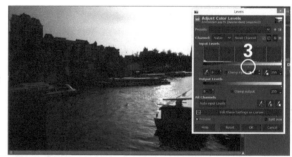

If you drag the middle slider to the left, the image brightens up (2). And if you drag it to the right, the image darkens (3). I want to brighten the image up.

So what do the two black sliders and the two white sliders do? The top black slider makes dark colors darker, and the top white slider makes light colors lighter. So when is this necessary?

Let's have a look at how the program can help us with that question. Open *Mountains.jpg*, and open Levels again.

The graph we see here is called a *histogram* (4). The *histogram* shows us how *many* dark pixels there are in the image, up until how *many* light pixels there are in the image. Our histogram shows that this image *doesn't* have colors in the *brightest* area (5).

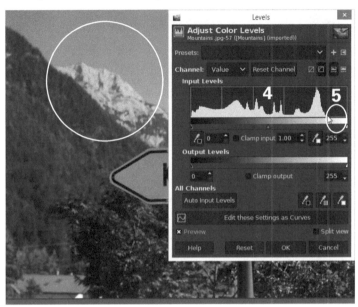

So what can we do with this information? If we want to introduce more *bright* colors in the image (and we do, to get the snow more white), we can drag the white slider to the point where the histogram *ends* (6).

Now we let our eyes decide if this improves our image. On the bottom left you have a *Preview* button (7). By clicking on it, you can compare the before and after. I think this improves the image. The snow on the mountain has become white (isn't greyish anymore).

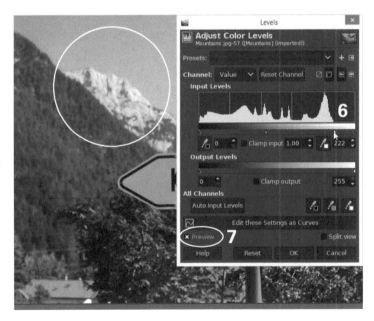

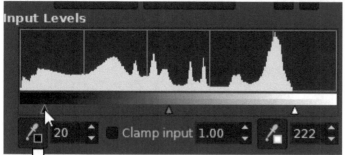

Now what about the black slider? As we can see in the histogram, the image doesn't mis any dark colors (there are colors up until the deepest blacks). So what would happen if we drag the black slider to the right, *inside* the colors of the histogram? What then happens is called **clipping**. All the darkest colors inside your image, that find themselves at the *left* side of the *black* slider, will now become *completely black* (8). Their *Value* will become 0. So *clipping* means *losing* visual information in either the shadows or highlights, although it may not always be that noticeable. So *Value* adjustments with the top *black* and top *white* slider can sometimes be a trade-off between getting a desired overall *Value* effect, and having some clipping. Most of the time however, dragging the black and white slider to the point where the graph ends (as we did with the white slider to get the snow white), is enough to get an *optimal* and *balanced* result. Thereby, a *solútion* for clipping can be using *Curves*, which we will look at in the next lesson.

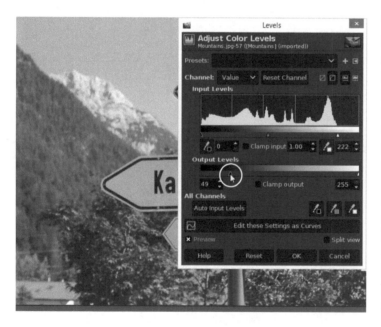

The bottom black and white sliders work in the opposite way as the top black and white sliders. Where the top black slider makes dark colors *darker*, the bottom black slider makes dark colors *lighter*. This will make the image look a bit washed out.

And where the top white slider makes light colors *lighter*, the bottom white slider makes light colors *darker*.
For correcting *Value*, the bottom black and white slider are seldom used.

You can also use Levels to change color, so; *Hue*. Open *Color_cast.xcf*. Here we have an image with a reddish color cast (the image looks red). Why is this? If you open the *Channels* panel, and look at the channels, you can see the Red channel is much *lighter* than the other two channels. This means there is much more red, than green and blue in the image. If we think back of the flashlights and the *unilluminated* wall, here the battery of the red *flashlight* (which is the red *channel*) is ok, but the green and blue flashlights don't give as much light (like their batteries are almost empty). As a result, the red flashlight *predominates*, which imbalances the color of the image.

We will now look at *three ways* to get the three channels at an equal level (to get all batteries *fully* charged).

For the *first* method, I will *darken* the red channel, to get the brightness of the three channels equal, which will remove the color cast. When the color cast is gone, I will brighten up *all three* channels at the same time, so, equally. Let's have a look.

Open *Levels*. If we look behind *Channel*, we see we are by default adjusting the *Value* (9). This *actually* means, we're adjusting the Value of *all three color channels* at the *same time* (so for red, green, and blue equally). You can however also adjust a *single* color channel *separately*.

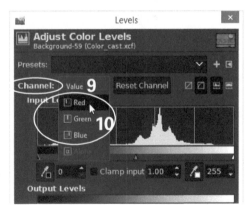

If you click on *Value*, you can see the *Red*, *Green* and *Blue* channels (10). Changing the Value for a *single* color channel, will change the color, or *Hue*, of the image!

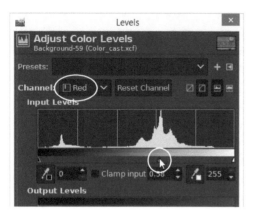

Because the *Red* channel is lighter than the other two channels, we will first *darken* the *Red* channel, in order to remove the color cast.

Choose the *Red* channel. To darken the Red channel, drag the middle slider to the *right*, until the image doesn't look red anymore. The image as a *whole*, has become darker now. To adjust this, go back to *Value* (to adjust the Value of the *three color channels at the same time*) and brighten the image up, by dragging the middle slider this time to the *left*.

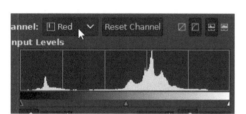

For the *second* method, we will look at the *histograms* of each channel *separately*. To go back to the *original* red image, you can use the *History* panel, or you can go to: *File > Revert* (this brings the image back to how it was when you opened it).

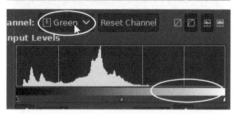

Open Levels. When you hold your mouse *above* Value, you can *scroll* with your mouse to look at the individual histograms of the three channels. We can see that the *Green* and *Blue* channel, are missing a lot of *highlights*.

I could manually optimize each channel (by dragging the *black* and *white* sliders to *fit* the *histograms*), but Gimp will do this *for* me. When you click on the *Auto Input Levels* button (10), all three histograms are *optimized*.

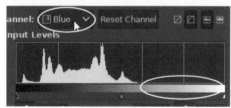

We see that by pressing a *single* button, we're able to remove almost *all* of the color cast.

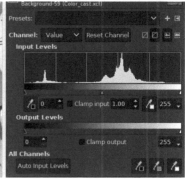

For the *third method*, we will use the three *Value pickers* at the right side of the *Auto* button. They are the **black point** (11), the **grey point** (12), and the **white point** (13) picker.

You can use just one, two, or all three of them. Let's start with the *white point picker* at the right. I select it. The place where I *click* on in the image, will become completely white (it's like the top *white slider* of the *histogram* is placed at *that* Value point). I can *click* in the sky, but I can also just *drag* in the sky, so I can quickly see different results.

Making the *sky white*, results in a somewhat *yellowish* image. This probably means that the sky *wasn't neutral white* when this picture was made, but probably had some *blue* in it.

So let's try another light point, for example on a light point on the sign (14). Now the result looks good.

Let's move on to the *grey point picker*. Finding a grey point can be difficult because we're not sure what area in the image was originally

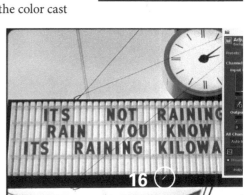

neutral grey. So I will experiment again. Although it is a bit dark, clicking at the center of the hands of the clock (15) seems to neutralise the color cast *even more*, so I will use this area.

And lastly, I select the *black point picker*. For the black point picker, I will look for a very *dark shadow area*, like the *bottom* of the sign board (16). The result looks good now.

In the next lesson we will meet Levels big brother: Curves.

17. Curves

In many cases, Levels will give you the result you're looking for. However, if you need more control, *Curves* will give you that. Open *Amsterdam.jpg* again. Go to: *Colors > Curves*.
In Curves, you can *create* as many 'sliders' as you want, *yourself*.
By *default*, you have a black (1) and a white (2) *point*, which are the little circles at the bottom and the top of the line. Now we are going to *add* a point ourselves (3), to recreate the *midpoint* slider we have in *Levels*.

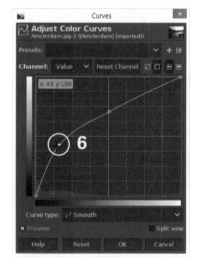

To add a point, just click somewhere on the line. Now that we have created a third point (our midpoint), how do we *use it* to darken or lighten the image?
Instead of dragging to the *left* and the *right* (as in Levels), in *Curves* you drag the points *up* and *down*. Dragging *down* (4) makes the Value point *darker*, and dragging *up* (5) makes it *lighter*. We can see all points are connected with a smooth curved line.

I will place another point, and drag it up to brighten the image in the *darker* areas (6).

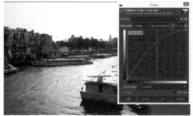
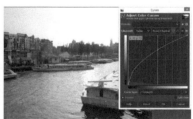

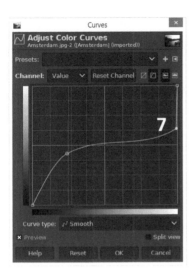

You can delete a point again by dragging it out of the window, at the *left* or *right* (7) side.

If there is a specific *area* in the image you want to adjust, for example the sky, you can add a point by *Shift-clicking* on this area (8).

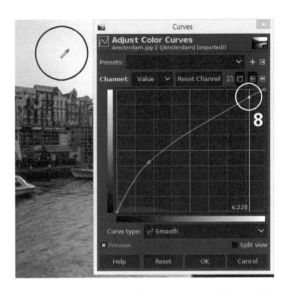

An *easy* way to *move* a point is by using the *up* and *down* arrow keys. To move a point in larger steps, hold down the *Shift* key while using the *up* and *down* arrow keys. To select *another point* on the curve, you can use the *left* and *right* arrow keys.

You can also make the window larger, by dragging at a corner or side (9).

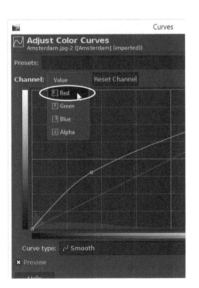

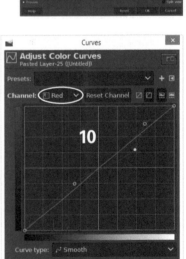

As with Levels, in Curves you can also adjust the *individual color channels*. This way, you can do sophisticated color corrections by adjusting the *individual* curves of the three color channels (10).

In the next lesson we will look at Brightness-contrast.

18. Brightness-Contrast

In this lecture we will look at *Brightness-Contrast*, and the special relationship between *Brightness-contrast*, *Levels* and *Curves*. Open *Tree.xcf*. Here we see the bark of a tree. The image looks a bit flat (1). It could use some more contrast. Go to: *Colors > Brightness-Contrast*. I increase the contrast a bit, to 30 (2). You can also do this by holding the mouse above the slider, and scroll. To compare, click on *Preview*.

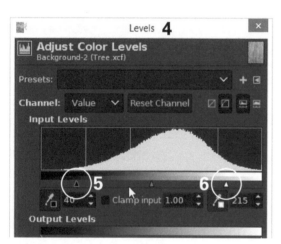

I you click on: *Edit these Settings as Levels* (3), *Levels* opens (4). Levels now shows what actually happened when we increased the contrast. The dark tones have been darkened (5), and the light tones have been lightened (6). The midtones have stayed unchanged. In *Levels*, I can click on *Edit these Settings as Curves*. Now I can see how my contrast adjustment looks like in *Curves* (7). I click on Cancel.

I open *Brightness-Contrast* again. I will now go the other way, and *reduce* the contrast by dragging the slider to the left. This results in a more flat, greyish image. To see what happened, click on *Edit these Settings as Levels* (8).

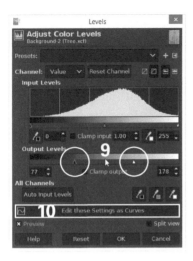

We can see that now the *Output* Levels sliders are brought inwards, making dark less dark, and light less light (9).

Click on *Edit these Settings as Curves* (10). This is how the contrast adjustment looks like in *Curves* (11). I click on Cancel.

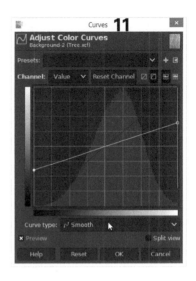

I open *Brightness-Contrast* one more time. We will now include the *Brightness* slider. When I increase the contrast, let's say to 40, the image gets lighter (12). I can adjust for this by *decreasing* the *Brightness* (13).

Click on *Edit these Settings as Levels*. What *Brightness* has done, is it has shifted *all three sliders* equally to the right, the midtone slider included (14).

To conclude, *Brightness-Contrast* is a quick and easy way to improve images that lack contrast. To fine-tune the result, you can go to *Levels* or *Curves*.

In the next lesson, we will look at *Hue-Saturation*.

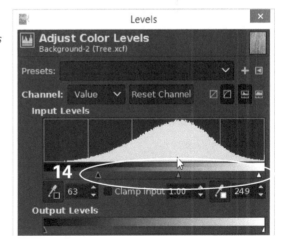

19. Hue-Saturation

As the name implies, with *Hue-Saturation* you can adjust two of the three color components; *Hue* and *Saturation*. In fact, you can even adjust *Value*, but not in the advanced way as you can with *Levels* or *Curves*. Each tool has its own speciality and unique way of working.
Open *Organ.jpg*.

Let's first look at *Saturation*. I would like to adjust the saturation of this image. To open *Hue-Saturation*, go to *Colors > Hue-Saturation*. I would like to bring a bit more color into this image. When you increase *Saturation*, you will shift pastel tints more to saturated colors. To do this, drag the *Saturation* slider to the right (1). If you toggle the *Preview*, you'll see the colors have come a bit more to life.

Hue-Saturation can also be used for color adjustments.
Click on *Reset* (2) to undo earlier settings. On top the color wheel is represented (3). The complementary color of *Red* (R), meaning the color on the *other side* of the color circle, is *Cyan* (C).
The complementary color of *Green* (G) is *Magenta* (M).
And the complementary color of *Blue* (B) is *Yellow* (Y).
In Hue-saturation you can *rotate* the color wheel. If you rotate, you're shifting the *Hue's*. You can do this for all colors at the same time, but also for *individual* colors.

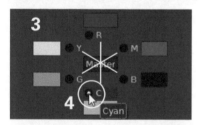

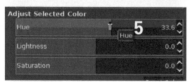

Let's say I want to make the pipes of the organ more blue.
Because the pipes are Cyan, I select *Cyan* (4) in the color wheel. I can now rotate the color wheel in two directions; *clockwise* and *counter clockwise*. If you rotate the color wheel clockwise, you'll move all *Cyan* colors to the direction of *Green*, *Yellow*, or *Red*. And if you go *counter clockwise*, you'll move *Cyan* colors in the direction of *Blue*, *Magenta*, and *Red*. So to shift *Cyan* to *Blue*, you go *counter clockwise*. To do this, drag the *Hue slider* to the right (5).

The image changes as you drag. And in the color wheel, you can see the *Cyan* thumbnail has been changed to *Blue* (6). Click on *Preview* to compare (7, 8). Then click on OK.
Let's look at a second example. Open *Mountains.jpg*.

Let's make the red leaves green. I open *Hue-Saturation*.
To adjust the red leaves, I select *Red (R)* in the color wheel.
To shift *Red* to *Green*, we go counter clockwise. I can drag the Hue *slider* to the right, but I can also fill in *degrees* manually. A single color shift (for example from *Red* to *Yellow*) is *60 degrees*. Shifting *two* colors is *120 degrees*, and going to the complementary color on the other side, is *180 degrees*.
I want to shift *two* colors, so a *120 degree* shift. I select the text inside the *Hue* entry field, type *120*, and press Enter.

As we can see, right now *not all* our reds have changed (9). To adjust how *many* red *tints* are affected, you use *Overlap*. Increasing Overlap (10) will *expand* the range of red colors that are shifted. As you drag Overlap to the right, more and more red tints will become green (11). We've now also made the roof of the house green. To deal with this use a layer mask (lesson 28). And *advanced* ways of selecting are discussed in the *Google Nik collection* chapter. All leaves are green now, but a bit too saturated. So I will *decrease* the *Saturation* by dragging the slider to the left. To get a better color match with the other green leaves in the image, I will shift the color a bit more to yellow, and set *Hue* to *90 degrees*. We've now changed red leaves into green leaves.

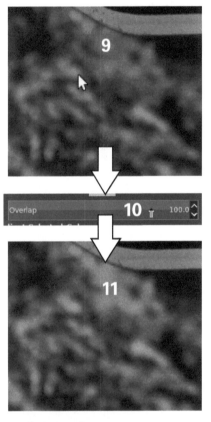

For the last example open *Girl.jpg*. The girl wears a blue shirt. Let's make the shirt darker. Click on *Blue (B)* in the color wheel. Increase *Overlap* to include all blue tints. Now I drag *Lightness* to the left to darken the shirt. I'll also decrease the *Saturation* a bit. To change the *color* of the shirt, drag the *Hue* slider.

In the next lesson we will look at the Color Picker.

20. Color Correction tools

In Gimp 2.10 some new color tools have been added.
Open Girl_summer. I open *Color Temperature*.

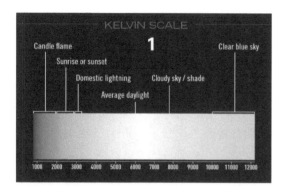

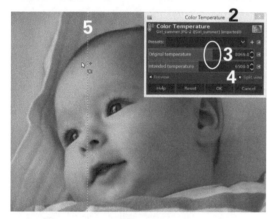

The human eye is very good at removing color casts. Our eyes will compensate for the changes in color temperature, so that white objects quickly look white to our eyes although objectively they are not. A camera isn't always as good at compensating for changes in color temperature as our eyes, which is why a camera sometimes captures a bit cooler or warmer colors than we perceived it.

Color temperature objectively is described in Kelvin, and ranges from 1,000 Kelvin to 12,000 Kelvin (1). Higher color temperatures are more bluish, so 'cooler' colors, and lower color temperatures are more orange, so 'warmer' colors. When an image looks a bit to warm or to cold, we can correct this with *Color Temperature* (2).

My image is a little too warm, so I drag the slider a bit to the right (3). When I click on *Preview*, I see I have a bit more natural skin tone. With *'Split view'* (4), you can drag a line (5) to quickly compare the before and after in a specific area.

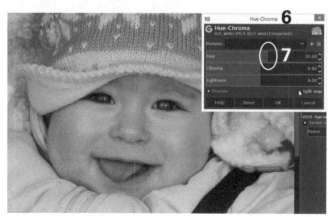

Now open Girl_winter. This image is taken in the winter. The skin looks a bit purplish, however, there isn't an overall color cast. This is why *Color Temperature* will not bring a solution. But with Gimp's new *Hue-Chroma* (6) filter I can quickly remove the purple from the skin, by dragging Hue to the right (7). By activating *'Split view'*, I can compare the left and right side of the face.

And lastly let's look at the new and powerful *Shadows-Highlights* filter. Open Dark_shadow. I open *Shadows-Highlights* (8).

This image has some very dark shadows, that are not recoverable with Levels or curves. When I drag *'Shadows'* to the right (9), the shadows are lightened up. This filter works for some images, like this one, and for some it won't. For those images it doesn't work, you can use the *Shadow-Adjustments* slider of *Viveza* plugin, which is described in the *Nik Collection* chapter.

In the next lecture we'll look at the *Color Picker*.

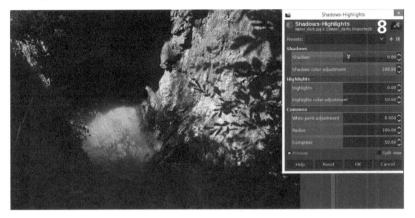

21. Using the Color Picker

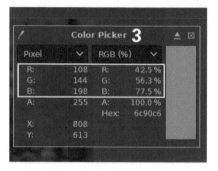

With the *Color Picker* you can sample or pick a color from your image. Open *Girl.jpg*. Select the *Color Picker* tool (1). If you click on the shirt (2), the *Foreground color* will show the sampled color.

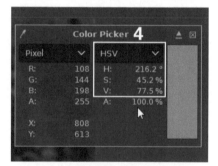

If you *Shift-click* on the image, the *Color Picker window* opens (3). At the left there are the *Red*, *Green* and *Blue* values from 0 to 255, and at the right, Red, Green and Blue are shown as *percentages*.

You can also show *Hue*, *Saturation* and *Value* if you want to (4). If you *drag* in your image you'll see the color information directly updated.

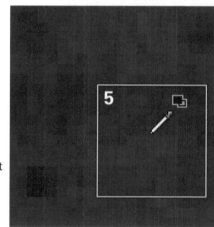

At the end of the Color Picker, there is a little *white square*. Let's zoom in to see the square better (5). The color you sample with the *Color Picker*, is an *average* of the pixels that are *inside* the square. The reason for this, is that pixels lying next to each other can *differ* quite a bit. Taking an *average* of a couple of pixels will give a more reliable result.

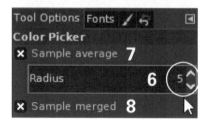

The size of the square can be adjusted in the *Tool Options*. The *Radius* (of the square) is now set to 5 (6). A *Radius* of 5 means we'll get an 11 by 11 pixel *square*. This is also a default size in Photoshop. To change the *Radius*, you can scroll inside the Radius bar. If you want to sample just a *single* pixel, uncheck *Sample average* (7).

Sample merged (8) means, that *all layers* are looked at, when you click somewhere. So not just the active layer is measured, but *all visible layers*. This means you're measuring what you're actually seeing.

In the next lesson we will look at how to save a file with layers.

22. Saving work file

To save a file that has layers, you save it in Gimp's native *.xcf* format. You can later open this 'work' file again, and continue working with the layers. To save a work file, go to: *File > Save As*. The *Save Image* window opens (1). At the top you can give your file a name (2), and at the left you can navigate to the folder

where you want to save (3). Then click on Save (4).

If you want to create a new folder, you can do this by clicking on the *Create Folder* button at the top right (5). As we saw earlier, you can also (6) *bookmark* a folder. Bookmarked folders are time savers for *both* opening and

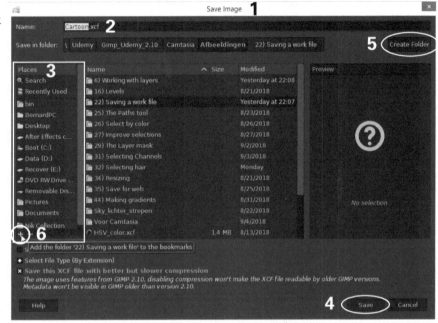

saving files. Because we are saving in Gimps native format, Gimp by default only shows existing *.xcf* files that are in a folder. If you want to see all the images in a folder, click at the bottom right on: *Show All Files* (7).

In chapter 4 we will look at saving images for the Web, for Print, saving as a PDF, and saving as a Photoshop file.

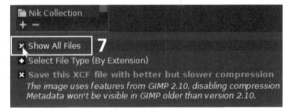

In the next Chapter we will look at making *selections*.

Chapter 3

Making selections

23. The Rectangle and Ellipse select tool

In this lecture, we'll look at the *Rectangle* (1) and *Ellipse* (2) select tool. If I want to brighten up the sky in a landscape, and leave the *rest* of the image untouched, I need a way to *select* the sky. In this chapter we will look at different ways to make a *selection*. We will start with two elementary, but important selection tools: the *Rectangle* and the *Ellipse* select tool. They can be found at the top and bottom of the *Tool bar*.
Let's create a new document. Go to: *File > New*. Make it 800 by 500 pixels (3). Click on the *Rectangle* tool at the top (4), or press *M*.

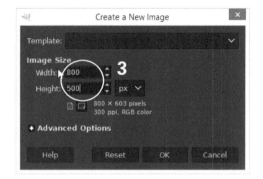

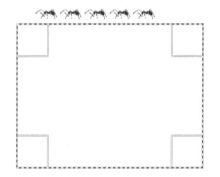

To draw a selection, *drag* over the canvas. You can recognize a selection because of the 'marching ants', as they are called. The marching ants define the *border* of the selection. Everything that is *inside* the selection, is *selected*, everything that is *outside* the selection, is *not selected*. Press *Enter* to confirm the selection. Now that we have a selection, what can we do with it? Let's open *Levels* by going to: *Colors > Levels*. If I now drag the white *output* slider to the left, only the pixels *inside* the selection will be darkened (5). The pixels *outside* the selection are unaffected. Click on Cancel.
To *stop* a selection, go to: *Select > None*, or press *Ctrl-D*. The *D* in *Ctrl-D*, stands for 'De-select'.
The marching ants are gone, and there is no selection anymore.

Let's explore the *Rectangle* tool a bit further. Drag a selection again. You can now *change* the *size* of the selection by dragging at the sides (6), or by dragging at the corners (7).

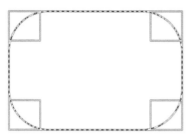

To get rounded corners, in the *Tool Options*, click on *Rounded corners* (8). With *Radius* you determine the *size* of the rounded corners. Press *Enter* to confirm the selection. Press *Ctrl-D* to deselect.

Now let's have a look at the *Ellipse* select tool, which is at the bottom of the toolbar. Click on it, and drag an ellipse. Here we can also change its size by dragging at the sides and the corners. Press *Ctrl-D* to deselect.

To daw a perfect *circle*, first start dragging, and then add the *Shift* key (9). Keep the *Shift* key pressed down. When you're finished dragging, *first* release the mouse button, and then release the *Shift* key. This works the same for the *Rectangle* select tool to create a square.

You can also *move* your selection, by dragging *inside* the selection. Clicking inside the selection *without moving* the selection, is the same as pressing *Enter*. This will turn the *adjustable* selection into a *normal* selection (10). A normal selection cannot be adjusted by dragging at the sides or the corners. However, when you click *inside* the selection *again* with the *Rectangle* (or *Ellipse*) select tool, you will be able to drag the sides and corners again (11).

If you have made a selection, and then press *Shift*, at the right of the cursor you will see a *small plus sign* appearing (12). By holding down *Shift*, you can now *add another* selection (13). You can move *and* adjust the second selection *independent* of the first selection. If you want to *merge* the two selections *together*, drag the new selection *over* the first selection (14).

You can now still do some last adjustments to it (15), and when you want to merge, press *Enter* to confirm (16).

Now the two selections have merged to one selection.

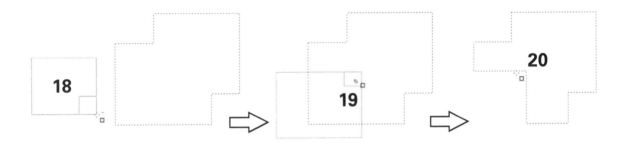

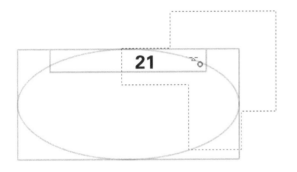

You can also *subtract* from a selection. If you press *Ctrl*, at the right of the cursor you will see a *small minus sign* appearing (17). With *Ctrl* pressed down, drag a new selection (18). You can drag the new selection *over* the existing selection. You can make some last

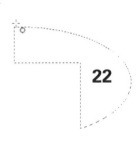

adjustments (19), and press *Enter* (20). You have now *subtracted* from the selection.

You can also make an *intersection*. Let's use the *Ellipse* select tool for this. Press *Shift plus Ctrl*, and drag *over* the existing selection. You can make some last adjustments (21), and then press *Enter*. Now you made an *intersection* of the two selections (22).

You can *undo* selection changes, by pressing *Ctrl-Z*. Each selection change is a *separate* state in the *History* panel (23).

Now we've seen how to create different shapes with selections, in the next lesson we will look at the *Free select* tool.

24. The Free select tool

With the *Free select* tool, you can freely draw selection shapes by hand. Click on the *Free select* tool that looks like a *lasso* (1).

To draw a shape, drag (2), and when you return to the beginning of your shape, you will see a yellow circle (3). When your mouse is above the yellow circle, release your mouse, and the shape *closes*. To turn the shape into a *selection* press *Enter* or *double-click inside* the shape. Press *Ctrl-D* to deselect.

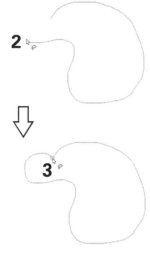

Another way to draw with the *Free select* tool is by *clicking*. Click once on the canvas to start a new shape. If you now move your mouse you'll get a *straight line*. Click again, and move your mouse again. To make a *horizontal* or *vertical* line (4), press the *Ctrl* key. Another way to close a selection, is by *double-clicking*. From wherever you double-click, you will *close* the selection with a straight line (5).

You can *both* drag *and* click interchangeably, while making a selection.

As with the *Rectangle* and *Ellipse* select tool, you can *add* to the selection, or *subtract* from it. And this is where the Free select tool is often used for. With the Free select tool you can quickly correct and optimize an existing selection. When you hold down *Shift*, you *add* to the selection (6). And when you hold down *Ctrl*, you *subtract* from the selection (7). Always press *Enter* to confirm.

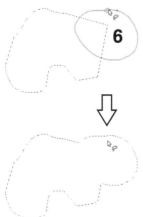

So with the *Free select tool*, you can quickly make a selection in any form.

In the next lesson, we will discover the *Path* tool, which is the tool for making professional selections.

25. The Paths tool

The contour of real world objects such as people, flowers, or cars, exists of mainly curved lines. To accurately select these curves, we use the *Paths* tool. The *Paths* tool can be found at the left side of the *Text* tool (1). Open *Sine.xcf*.

We'll explore the paths tool by drawing over a curved line. I start at the top left. I click and hold the mouse button down (2). Now I drag a bit to the right (3). What I just did is, I placed a point (which is the circle in the middle) and by dragging I pulled *out* of the circle *two arms*. The circle is the center, and the arms can be *rotated* around it. The arms can also be pulled out and pulled in.

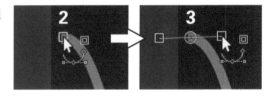

The function of the arms is to give the line we are going to draw *curvature*. Let's place a second point at the bottom of the sine. Click (4), and drag to the right again (5). As we see, by dragging out the arms, we're adjusting the curvature of the line.

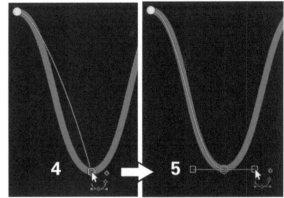

Release the mouse button. If you want to, you can now move *each* arm *individually* (6).
And when you press *Shift*, the arms will move as *one* again, mirrored in their origin point (the circle).

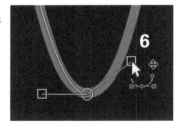

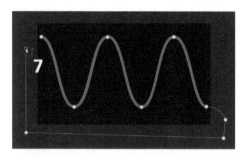

To *close* a path (7), press *Ctrl* (8) and click on the first placed point (9).

After closing a path you can *still* improve the path by dragging all points, and adjusting all arms.

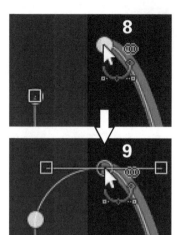

Open *Circle.xcf*. To quickly draw a path around the circle, I will first place four points without dragging, one point at every 90 degrees (10). To help placing these four points, two lines are visible in the circle. To close the path, *Ctrl*-click on the first point. Next, add four *additional* points in the middle of the straight lines. To *add* a new point on a line, press *Ctrl*, and *click on the line* (11). A new point will be added. Drag the new point to the edge, about in the middle (12). To make the curve *fit* the circle, press *Shift* and drag the arms out just a bit further (13).

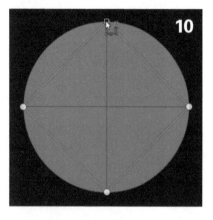

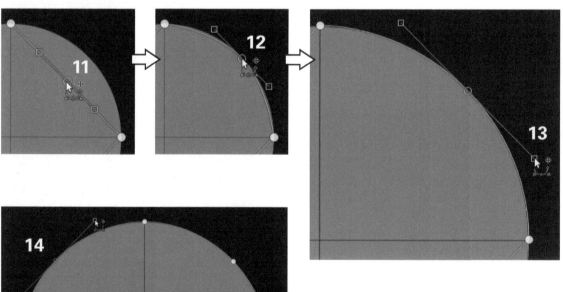

Also do this for the other three lines (14). Now our path is finished.

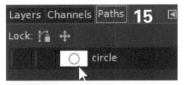

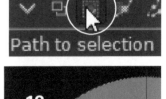

After drawing a path, we want to get a *selection* from it. To turn a path into a *selection*, go to the *Paths* panel (15). Here you can see a thumbnail of the path you drew. Like in the layers panel, you can give the path a name. I call it *circle*.

To turn the path into a selection, click on the *Path to selection* icon (16). Now we see the marching ants again (17). You can *hide* the path (so you will *only* see the *selection*) by clicking on the *Move* tool (18). Deselect by pressing *Ctrl-D*. To make the *path* visible again, and *automatically* also select the *Path* tool, just *double*-click on the path *thumbnail*.

Now let's create a *second* path, by *Shift*-clicking on the *Create a new path* icon (19). I draw a simple triangle, partly *over* the circle, and close the path by *Ctrl*-clicking on the first point (20). In the Paths panel, when you *Alt*-click on the *circle thumbnail*, éven though this path is *not* selected *or* visible, *Alt*-clicking will give you it's selection. Like with the *Rectangle* and *Ellipse* select tools, you can *add*, *subtract*, or *intersect* with a second selection, *now* coming from a *path*. This means we can *add* the *triangle* selection *to* the circle selection by *Shift-Alt* clicking on the triangle thumbnail (21).

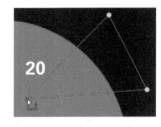

We have now *added* the *triangle* to the *circle*, as a selection (22).

Let's also do an *intersection*. I create a third path by *Shift*-clicking on the *Create a new path* icon. I draw a *rectangle*, partly over the circle (23). To get an intersection of this *rectangle* with the *selection*, press *Shift-Ctrl-Alt*, and click on the *rectangle* thumbnail. To hide the path and *only* see the selection, click on the *Move* tool (24).

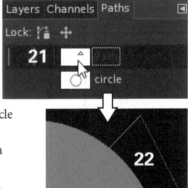

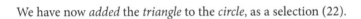

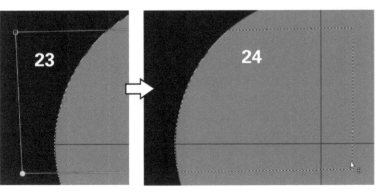

Now let's practice with a real image. Open *Coffee.xcf*. Let's say, in this image I would like to change the *color* of the background, but I want to leave the mug unchanged.

To do this I will select the mug by drawing a path around it. When the mug is selected, I will cut out the mug, and place the isolated mug on a separate layer on top. If I then change the color of the layer below, the mug won't be affected, because it has been placed on a separate layer.

Select the *Paths* tool, and zoom in to about 400%.

Here I recognize a *sine wave form* (25). I will click and drag my first point at the top of the sine (26). Then I click and drag at the bottom of the sine (27). To make the curve fit, I adjust the arms. The direction and length of the arms, will form the curve.

After adjusting, when you want to continue drawing, the *last placed point* has to be the *active point*. An active point has a *transparent* circle, instead of a circle filled with *white*. So when the last placed point is white, and you want to continue drawing, *click* on the last point to make it active (transparent). Then you can continue drawing.

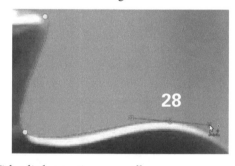

I click and drag a new point, and adjust the handles again (28).

When the distance between two points gets longer, the curve often will be more difficult to draw. However, placing points too close to each other, also isn't effective and will be time-consuming. With a little practice, you will quickly start to recognize the *natural* existing *sine forms*, so you won't draw more curves than needed, and you won't try to draw several curves at the same time.

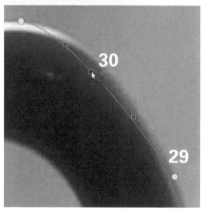

For larger areas I personally use the method I used for drawing the circle.

I click (so without dragging) to set a new point (29). At the place, where there is the *most* distance between my line, and the edge of the object, I will *Ctrl*-click to place a new point (30). Then I drag this point to the edge. To *continue* drawing, *first* click on the *last* point to make it active.

After finishing, we have a path *around* the mug. We however should not forget the *inside* of the handle. Drawing a new path, *inside* a path, will automatically *exclude* this area from the selection (31). Now our path is complete (32).

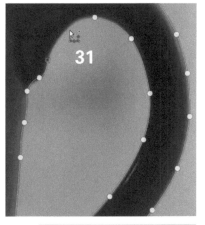

In the Paths panel *Alt*-click on the thumbnail, to turn the path into a selection (33). Press *V* to select the *Move* tool, so you only see the selection (34).

Now open the layers panel. To place the mug on a new layer, press *Ctrl-J*. After pressing *Ctrl-J*, the selection is

gone, and the content of the selection is placed on a new layer, *above* the layer that was active. The new layer will have the name: *Layer via Copy*, and it will be the active layer.

In the Layers panel, you are *also* able to *Alt*-click on a layer thumbnail. The selection you get will come from the *existing pixels* that are on that layer. *Alt*-clicking on the *Layer via Copy* layer, will give the same selection as *Alt*-clicking on the mug *path*. Also, like in the Paths panel, a layer *doesn't* have to be selected *or* visible, to get a selection from it.

In the *Layers* panel we're also able to *add*, *subtract*, and *intersect* selections (based on the existing pixels on a layer). The same key combinations are used: *Shift-Alt* clicking will *add* the pixels of a layer to the selection. *Ctrl-Alt*-clicking will *subtract* the pixels of a layer, from the selection. *Shift-Ctrl-Alt* clicking will give an *intersection* of the pixels on a layer, and the selection.

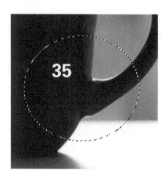

I make a circle selection (35).
Then I *Shift-Alt*-click on the mug layer, to *add* the selection of the mug.

I make a circle selection again. Now I *Ctrl-Alt*-click on the mug layer, to *subtract* the mug *from* the *circle* selection (37).

I make a circle selection again. Now I *Shift-Ctrl-Alt*-click on the mug layer, to make an *intersection* of the *mug* and the *circle* selection (38). Deselect by pressing *Ctrl-D*.

With *Ctrl-J* we placed the mug on a separate layer, *above* the background. So I can now change the color of the background, without affecting the mug.

In the next lesson we'll explore how to select color.

26. The Select by color tool

In this lesson we will look at how to make a selection based on *color*.

In the toolbox there are *two* color select tools. They both do the same thing: they make selections based on color *similarity*. The *Fuzzy select* tool (1) looks for similar colors *adjacent* to where you click. The *Select by color* tool (2) looks *everywhere* in the image to find similar colors. Open *Coffee.xcf*. The *Fuzzy select* tool, known as the 'Magic Wand tool' in Photoshop, is located below the *Move* tool. Let's see if we can select the mug with the *Fuzzy select* tool. When you click somewhere on the mug, the tool will select colors that are *similar* to the color you clicked on. How different a color has to be before it is included in the selection, is set under *Threshold* in the *Tool Options*. The *higher* the Threshold, the *more* colors that will be included in the selection, and the *larger* the area of the selection will become. An efficient way to increase the Threshold is by dragging *inside the image*.

When you drag *inside the mug* (3), in the *Tool Options* the Threshold is going up (4). And as the Threshold is going up, more and more pixels are added to the selection. At some point however, the selection will go *outside* the mug (5). In an ideal situation, you would be able select the whole mug, before the selection goes outside the mug. However, objects in the real world are not always that easy to select by their color. With a partial selection the question arises: should I *use* this selection I have, and try to *improve* it, or am I better off by drawing a *path*? A third possibility is using the **Nik collection** which is specialised in making professional selections. We'll look at the Nik collection in chapter 5.

Open *Sky.jpg*. Let's say we want to select the sky. If you use the *Fuzzy select* tool and you drag in the sky, you're *not* selecting the blue sky *between* the *branches* of the tree (6). This is because the Fuzzy select tool only selects *connected* pixels, starting from the place where you start dragging. The other color selection tool is the *Select by Color* Tool. For the *Select by Color* tool, similar colors *don't* have to be connected, so you can get multiple selections. Click on the *Select by Color* tool. If you now drag in the image, the blue sky between the branches is also selected (7).

Fuzzy select

Select by Color

To include the cloud at the left, I use the *Free Select* tool.

To *add* to the selection, press the *Shift* key and click once. After having placed the first point, you can release the *Shift* key. Click around the cloud. You can also click *outside* the image, to include everything (8).

When you close the selection, you have *added* the cloud *to* the selection (9). With the selection loaded press *Ctrl-J*. Ctrl-J will place the selected sky on a separate layer (10). You can now adjust the sky.

If you need a *selection* of the sky again, you can *Alt*-click on the sky layer thumbnail. And when you need a new layer with the *original* sky, click on the background and press *Ctrl-J* again.

In the next lecture we'll look at ways to improve a selection.

27. How to improve selections

In this lecture, we will *improve* the selection we get from the mug, using the skills we have learned so far. Open *Coffee.xcf*.

Select the mug again (1), by dragging inside the mug (2) and selecting as much of the mug as possible (3). Now we will improve the selection, and use various methods for this.

There are three areas where we have to *add* to the selection. And *below* the mug the selection went outside the mug, so we have to *remove* the selection area there. To remove a big piece of a selection, you can use the *Rectangle select* tool. Press *Ctrl* to *subtract* from the selection, and start dragging from under the image up until the mug (4). Then press Enter (5).

Now select the *Free select* tool. Let's add the top of the mug to the selection. Press the *Shift* key to add, and click inside the selection (6). After placing the first point, you can release the *Shift* key.

Now go over the top of the mug, to add it to the selection (7). Because the *Free select* tool is unable to draw curves, you have to draw the curve at the top by placing several short distanced points (8).

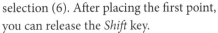

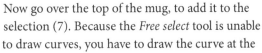

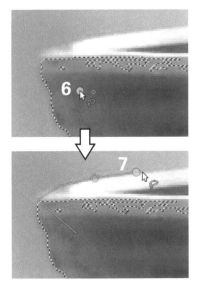

When you have reached the inside of the selection again (9), you can close the selection, for example by double-clicking. Then press *Enter* (10).

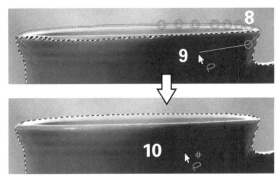

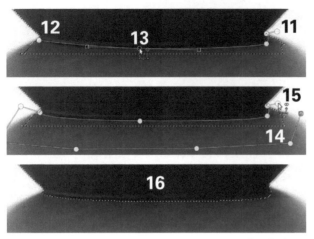

Because the *Free select* tool can't draw curves, I will now use the *Paths* tool to correct the bottom of the mug.

I select the *Paths* tool. I start the path somewhere outside the selection (11). To make a curve for the bottom, I place a point at the other side (12). Then I press *Ctrl*, and click in the middle to add a point. I drag the point to the edge (13). Then I hold *Shift* so I can move *both* arms at the same time, and drag the arms *out* to get the right curvature. I click on the end point to continue. To finish the path, I go outside the selection again (14). I close the path by *Ctrl*-clicking on the first point (15). I go to the *Paths* panel. I *subtract* the path from the selection, by *Ctrl-Alt* clicking on the path thumbnail. I press *V* to see the result (16).

You can also turn a *selection*, into a *path* (and then adjust the *path* instead of the selection). At the right side of the *Path to selection* icon, we have its *opposite*: the *Selection to path* icon (17). When you click on it you get a new path, called: Selection (18). Double-click on the path thumbnail, and deselect the selection by pressing *Ctrl-D*.

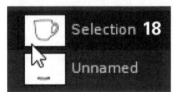

I zoom in on the path that was created from the selection. I can reposition points (19), and I can adjust the handles (20). Hold down *Ctrl* to be able to pull out the arms, when they are still *inside* a circle.

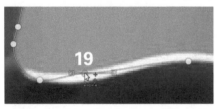

You can also *delete* points by selecting them, and pressing *Backspace*. When you're finished adjusting the path, *Alt*-click on the path thumbnail, to get a new selection. Press *V* to select the *Move* tool. Go to the *Layers* panel, and place the Mug on a new layer, by pressing *Ctrl-J*.

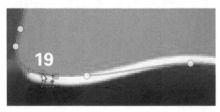

In the next lesson we will look at a powerful way to select: *painting* selections.

28. The Quick mask

Another way to make a selection, is by *painting* it. This is very useful for isolating objects that don't have a *hard edge*. Let's have a look. Open *Monkeys.jpg*. Because of the fur, the monkeys have a soft transition to the background. Drawing a path would be very difficult, and also *wouldn't* give a satisfactory result. For selecting soft edges, you use the *Quick mask*.

To prepare for the *Quick mask*, I will first make a *rough* selection with the *Free select* tool, at the outside of the monkeys (1). By holding down the mouse, I can quickly draw around them.

To go to the *Quick mask*, click at the bottom left on the little icon (2). You can also press *Q*. By pressing *Q*, you will toggle between *Quick mask mode*, and *selection mode*. In Quick mask mode you can now clearly see the *inside*, and the *outside* of the selection (3). The monkeys are at the *inside* of the selection. Everything that's outside the selection, is colored *red*. Like in Photoshop, *red* for the Quick mask is the default. But you can change this to another color, as we will see later.

Let's zoom in a bit, so we can clearly see the transition from the fur to the background. Select the *Paintbrush* tool, and select a soft brush with 0% hardness. Press *Alt* and scroll the brush size to around 60. Set the Fore- and Background to black and white, by pressing *D*. Painting with black will make the selection *smaller* (the *red* area is made bigger) and painting with white makes the selection *larger*. By pressing the *X* key, you can quickly *switch* between painting with black and painting with white. Let's start with black, to *hide* more of the background (4).

I will adjust the appearance of the mask a bit, to better see what I am painting. I right-click on the Quick mask *icon* at the bottom left, and choose: *Configure Color and Opacity* (5). To adjust the *color* of the Quick mask, click on the rectangle at the right (6).

The *Edit Quick Mask Color* window will open (7). You can now adjust the *color* of the Quick mask. I my situation the *red* gives good contrast with the *green* background, so I will keep the red. I click on Cancel. What I will change is the Mask *opacity*. When I *increase* the Mask *opacity* (8), the Quick mask becomes *less* transparent. This helps me to better see the result of my painting.

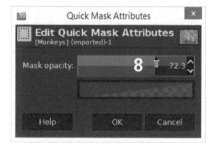

I drag the opacity slider to about 70%, and click on OK.

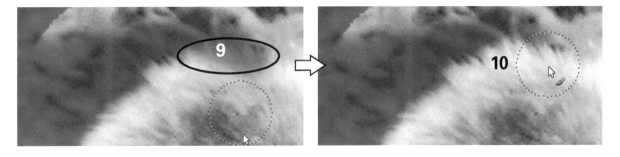

When you remove too much fur (9), just press *X* to reverse the brush. Then paint with white, to *increase* the selection again (10). At different places, you can use different brush sizes. For example, around the *nose* (11) of the right monkey, you can use a *smaller* brush, because there is almost no fur.

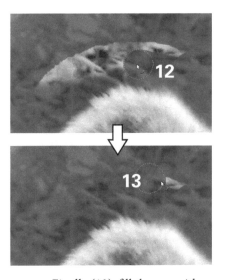

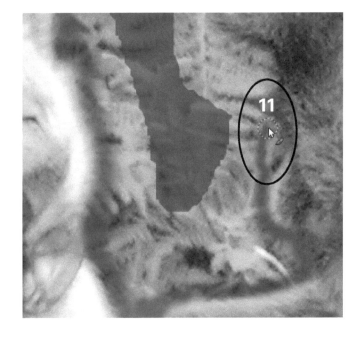

Finally (12), fill the gap with a hard brush (13).

When you're finished (14), press *Q* to go to *selection mode*. Then press *Ctrl-J* to place the selected monkeys on a new layer (15).

In the next lecture, we will look at a more flexible and *non-destructive* alternative for using *Ctrl-J*; the layer mask.

29. The Layer mask

Until now we have used *Ctrl-J* to place selected pixels on a separate layer. In this lecture, we will look at a *non-destructive* alternative for using *Ctrl-J*: the layer mask.

At the left side we see the *Ctrl-J* method (1). The bottom layer is the original image, shown with a selection around the monkeys (2). Pressing *Ctrl-J* will

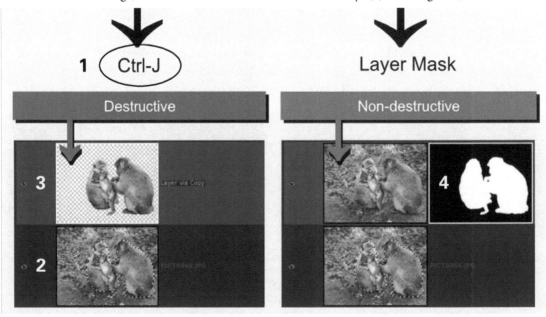

give us the layer above (3), as we did in the last lectures. When we use *Ctrl-J*, we *copy* the pixels inside of the selection, and place these pixels on the layer above (3). The pixels *outside* the selection are discarded.

This is called *destructive*, because we are *losing* pixels from a layer. Losing pixels from a layer also means *losing the ability* to make *changes later on*. For example, if I later would decide I also want to show the *twig* the baby monkey is holding, I can't do that anymore on the *Layer via Copy* layer, because the pixels I need for this, are not available anymore. So ideally, I would leave *all* the existing pixels of a layer intact, when I *isolate* an object. I can do this, by using a layer *mask*, which is shown at the right (4).

A layer *mask* is a second, black and white image, that is *added* to a layer. A layer mask will *store the selection* that you make. Where the mask is *white*, you will see the *content* of the layer, and where the mask is *black*, the content of the layer is *hidden* (white *reveals*, black *conceals*). This way, no pixels have to be deleted. They are just *hidden* by the mask. The mask is very flexible, because you can show and hide content of a layer, *at any time*.

A layer mask can also have tints of *grey*. Where the mask is *grey*, the layer has *transparency*. A darker grey (5) means *more* transparency, so the content here will only be slightly visible (6). And a lighter grey (7) means *less* transparency, so the content will be more visible (8) but is still transparent, so *you can still* see through it.

If I now want to add the *twig* that the baby monkey is holding, I am able to do that by changing the *black* pixels on the layer mask, to *white* pixels. This will reveal the twig. I could draw a *path* around the twig, turn that path into a *selection*, and fill the selection with *white*, *inside* the layer mask, which reveals the twig.

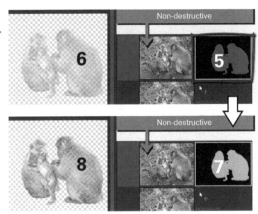

Open *Monkeys_twig.xcf*. Here *Ctrl-J* has been used to create the top layer. At the bottom we have the original layer. On the original layer, we are going to place a layer mask. First *Alt*-click on the top layer to get a *selection* from its pixels (its content). Then *right-click* on the bottom layer, and choose: *Add Layer Mask* (9). You can also click on the *Add a mask* icon (10).

We want to make a mask from the *selection*, so click on *Selection* (11). Then press Enter.

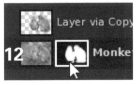

We can now see, an extra black and white thumbnail has been added at the right side of the content thumbnail (12). The black and white mask has now *stored* our selection, so you can safely *deselect* the selection by pressing *Ctrl-D*. The *Ctrl-J* layer and *mask* layer now *visually* show exactly the same content. However, on the *Ctrl-J* layer the non-visible pixels have been *deleted*, and on the *mask* layer the non-visible pixels are just *hidden*, and can be revealed at any time.

To add the twig, I've already made a path (13). Go to the *Paths* panel, and *Alt*-click on the twig thumbnail to turn the path into a selection. Go back to the *Layers* panel. To add the twig, make sure that the black and white *mask* is *selected*. You can see whether the mask is selected, by the *white border* around the mask thumbnail (12). The layer *content* thumbnail now has a *black border* (12), which indicates it is *not* selected.

If you click on the *content* thumbnail, you'll see the white border is now around the *content* thumbnail (14). Click on the *mask* again (15). To fill the mask with white (coming from the selection) press *Ctrl-Backspace* (16). Press *Ctrl-D* to deselect. We now made the twig *visible* on the content layer (17).

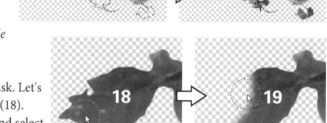

You can also *paint* on the mask. Let's say we want to *remove* a leaf (18). Press *B* to select the brush, and select a soft brush. Set the size to about 50. Check that the *mask* is selected, so that you're not painting with black on the *content*. Paint with *black*, to *hide* pixels. When you now paint over the leaf (19), you are hiding it. This is because you're making white pixels black, inside the layer mask. Now let's *add* a leave.

To add a leave, I would like to have the background *visible* again, like I had with the *Quick mask*. To *simulate* the Quick mask, duplicate the layer with the layer mask. *Right-click* on the bottom layer mask layer, and choose: *Delete Layer Mask*. *Shift*-click on the *Create a new layer* button. Click on the Foreground color, select red, and click on OK. Press *Alt-Backspace* to fill the layer with red (20). Set the Opacity of the red layer, to 50% (21). Now click on the layer mask of the top layer (22). The Quick mask has now been simulated.

Like with the Quick mask, painting with *black* will make the selection *smaller*, and painting with *white* will make the selection *larger*. Press *D* to set the Fore- and Background to black and white. We can now easily *reveal* a leaf, because we're able to *see* the *hidden* pixels (because we placed the original image below, tinted red by a transparent red layer above it).

I'll paint with white, inside the *mask*. To get white press *X*, to switch the Fore- and Background color. I zoom in on the image to about 400%. Probably the easiest way to add a leaf, is by first *roughly* revealing what you want to add (so making *more* visible than is needed). Then (as we did with the monkeys) paint backwards with *black* towards the edge. At any time, you can *check* the result, by *Shift-clicking* on the eye of the top layer, which will then hide the layers below. *Shift*-click again, to reveal all layers again. For fine-tuning, you could paint with only the top layer visible.

Because we only *simulated* the Quick mask, pressing *Q* now *won't* give me a selection. To get a *selection* from the *mask*, *right-click* on the layer, and choose: *Mask to Selection* (23).

You can *hide* the mask, so temporarily disable it, by *Ctrl*-clicking on the mask (24). You can *see* a mask is *disabled*, when it has a *red* border around it. *Ctrl*-click on the mask again, to activate it again.

As you can hide a *mask*, you can also hide the *content* of a layer, so you only see the mask. To only see the mask, you *Alt*-click on the mask (25).

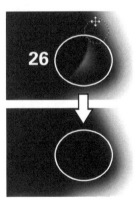

This can be useful to *check* the mask for small *mistakes*. Looking only at the mask, you can quickly see if you have missed a spot somewhere (26). You can *see* the *content* is hidden, when the mask shows a *green* border. *Alt*-click on the mask again to reveal the content again.

In the next lesson we will look at several common uses of layer masks.

30. Uses of Layer masks

Masks have many uses. They can for example be used for *Color* and *Value* corrections.

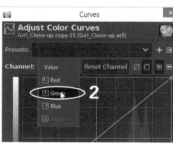

Open *Girl_Close-up.xcf*. Let's say I would like to remove the greenish color tint around the girls mouth (1). To do this, I first *duplicate* the layer, and then open *Curves*. I go to the *Green* channel (2).

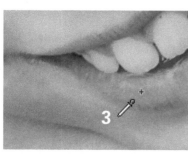

I now *Shift*-click (3) on the greenish skin. This will place a point in the Green channel at the *Value level* I want to adjust (4). Now I move the placed point *down* a bit, to *remove* green at this Value level (5). You can also use the *down* arrow key to lower the point (it's a bit easier than using the mouse). I click on OK.

Next, add a layer *mask* to the color adjusted layer. *Right-click* on the layer and choose *Add Layer Mask*. Choose *Black* for the color of the mask, so that you will start with *hiding* the complete layer (6). Press Enter. The layer is now hidden.

Press *B* to select the brush. Press *X* to paint with *white*, so you will *reveal* the pixels of the color corrected layer. Select a soft brush with 0% hardness. *Alt*-scroll to set the size to around 70. Now paint with a very *low brush opacity*. If you do this, you're able to *gradually* remove the green tint. Set the opacity of the brush to about 10% (7). With each paint stroke, you're

removing a bit of green where you paint, because you're *slowly adding* the color of the adjusted layer. This way you're flexible in *how much* green you want to remove. At those places where you removed too *much* green you can

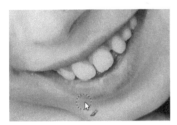

reverse the process by pressing *X*, and painting with *black*.

When you're satisfied with the result, you can *merge* the two layers back into *one* layer. You can do this by *right-clicking* on the top layer and choose: *Merge Down* (8). The shortcut for merging down is *Ctrl-E* (see also: *Layer > Merge Down*). We've now color corrected the image with the use of a layer *mask*.

Now we will look at *dodging and burning*, where we adjust the *Value* levels of an image, using layer masks. Make two copies of the layer you want to adjust (9). We will make one layer *darker*, and the other layer *lighter*. Open *Curves* to darken the top layer. Drag the curve down a bit, and click on OK. Call the layer 'darken'. Hide the top layer, and select the layer below. Open *Curves* again, to lighten this layer. Drag the curve up a bit, and click on OK. Call the layer 'lighten'.

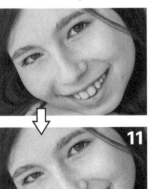

Now we will *hide* both Value adjusted layers with a (black) layer *mask*. *Right-click* on the layers, choose *Add Layer Mask*, choose *Black* for the color of the mask, and press Enter (10). Next select the brush. Choose a *soft* brush and increase the size to about 300. In the *Tool Options*, set the brush *Opacity* to around 30%. By painting inside the mask of the *darken* layer, you can *darken* areas. And when you paint inside the mask of the *lighten* layer, you can make areas *lighter* (11).

Finally we will look at two ways to create a *clipping mask*. You use a clipping mask when for example you want to see an image *inside* text. We will look at the method used *before* Gimp 2.10, and the new and improved method, that is used in Photoshop. We start with *Mask* clipping, which is the old method, and then we look at *Layer* clipping.

I have opened: Chicago. I would like to see the image of the city inside the text. Let's first look at *Mask* clipping. At the top we have a *text* layer (12). Using text will be discussed in the next chapter. Below, we have an image of a city. To make the city visible *inside* the letters, we'll use a *layer mask*. I *Alt-click* on the text layer, to get a selection of the text. Then I *right-click* on the Chicago layer, and choose: *Add Layer Mask* (13). I click on

Selection, and press Enter. I press *Ctrl-D* to deselect. I hide the text layer, so I can see the Chicago layer (14).

Now let's look at the three disadvantages of this method; *Mask* clipping. First, although I can reposition the *mask* independent from the image by dragging, I'm *not* able to move the *content* (the city) independent from the mask; the mask will move with it. Second, when I drag the mask *outside* the image (15) and back (16), the part that has been outside will be cut off. And third, when I want to change the text, I will have to make a *new* mask. Not ideal.

The solution is *Layer* clipping, which is now possible in Gimp 2.10. I *Control*-click on the *Add a mask* icon (17), to remove the layer mask.

For layer clipping, in Gimp we need a layer *group*. I click on the *Create a new Layer group* icon (18). I drag both the clipping layer (19), and the layer that will be clipped (20), in the *layer group*.

I place the image that will be clipped (so the visible content) on top (20) in the layer group, and the clipping layer (which is the text layer) below. Both layers must be visible.

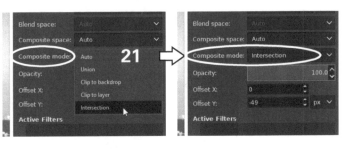

Now I *double-click* on the Chicago layer, and behind *Composite mode*, from the drop-down list I choose: *Intersection* (21). I click on OK.

I now can move the Chicago layer, *and* the clipping mask, which in this case is a text layer.
I can also move the clipping mask *outside* the canvas and back. And when I change the text, I don't have to make a new mask, because the text *is* the mask.
As we can see, *layer* clipping is an improvement over *mask* clipping.

We're also able, to *reverse* this effect. This means we can use the text to cut a hole in the image, so we can look through the image (there where is text). To do this I drag the text above the Chicago layer (22). Behind *Mode*, I choose *Erase* (23). I will hide the black layer to show the transparency we created.

Blending modes (like *Erase*) are discussed in the next chapter, but I already wanted to show you this trick here.
So with layer clipping, we made everything transparent *except* the text.
And with the *Erase* Blend Mode, we reversed the clipping: everything is visible *but* the text. Again, I can drag the text, drag the Chicago layer, and adjust the text (24).

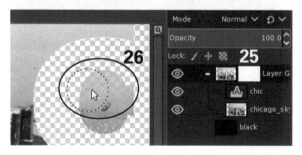

And finally you can also give a layer *group* a mask (25), which will let you further determine what is visible of the 'group content' as a whole. Here I make part of the group content semi-transparent (26), by painting with black in the mask with a lower brush opacity.

In the next lecture, we'll look at selecting channels.

31. Selecting Channels

In this lecture we'll look at how to make a selection from a Channel. Open *Channels.xcf*. I go to the *Channels* panel and set the size of the thumbnails to Enormous.
We have seen that layer masks are *black and white* images. The same is true for the Channels. The *Red*, *Green*, and *Blue* Channels are also *black and white* images. As we'll see in the next lesson where we will select hair, sometimes the information of a specific *Channel* can be very useful.

We see the numbers 1, 2, and 3. Each number is placed in a *separate* Channel. To turn the *Red* Channel (the 1) into a selection, *right-click* on it, and choose: *Channel to Selection* (1).

As we can see here, pure *black* pixels (in our case the number 1) aren't *included* in the selection (2). This is because in a selection, pure black *doesn't* have *any* transparency. As we saw with masks, *grey* pixels *do* have transparency. And white pixels are fully transparent. So *only* pure *black* pixels hide *completely*, and this is visually indicated by *excluding* black from the selection.

Let's say I want to use the *selection* of the *blue* channel (the 3), for making a layer *mask*. *Right-click* on the blue channel, and choose: *Channel to Selection* (3). To clearly see what is *inside* and what is *outside* the selection, you can also press Q to enter *Quick mask mode*. We see everything is selected, *except* the number 3 (because only the 3 is red). Press Q again to see the selection again.

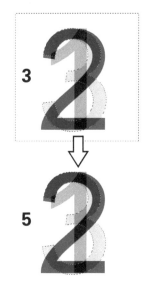

I want the number 3 as a selection, so I will need to turn the selection *around;* I need to *invert* the selection. To do this, I go to: *Select > Invert* (4). Now the number 3 is selected (5).

We have now made a *selection* of the blue channel, and we have *inverted* this selection.

Now, let's put the selection in to a layer *mask*. *Right*-click on the layer and choose: *Add Layer Mask*. Click on *Selection* (6), and press Enter. Press *Ctrl-D* to deselect. The layer mask is ready (7).

In the next lesson we will use this method to select hair.

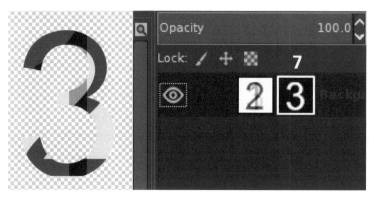

32. Selecting hair

In this lesson we'll look at how to select hair. Open *Girl_hair.xcf*. To select hair, we need to find the best contrast we can get, between the hair and its surroundings. To find the best contrast, we will compare the three Channels. Go to the *Channels* panel, and set the thumbnails of the Channels to Gigantic. In our case, even at Gigantic, I think the thumbnails are too small to clearly see the hair. A quick way to see the three Channels at 100% is by going to: *Colors > Components > Decompose*. Click on OK.

Gimp has made a new document, where the channels are now visible as *layers*, called red, green, and blue (1). Press *Ctrl-1* for a 100% view.

Now let's *compare* the layers to find the one that gives the *best contrast* between the hair and its surroundings. I think the blue layer gives the best contrast (2). So I will *drag* this layer *over* (3) to my original document (4). To do this, first drag the layer *on the thumbnail* of the original document, and then drag it *under the thumbnail*. We've now transferred a *layer* from one document, to another document.

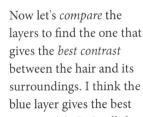

We have now two layers: a *color* layer on the bottom (5), and a *black and white* layer (which is the *blue* channel!) on top (6). We will use the *blue channel* layer, as a *mask* for the *color* layer. Masks and channels are both black and white, so this matches.

Before we can use the blue channel layer as a mask, we first have to adjust it. The *background* has to become completely *black*, so that as a mask, it will *hide* everything that's around the girl. And the girl itself has to become completely *white*, so she will be completely *visible*.

Right now however, the *hair* of the girl is *much darker* than the background (7). For this reason it is often easier to initially work the other way around. We will *first* make the girl and her hair black, and the background white. When we're finished refining the layer we will *invert* the layer (turn it into a negative), so black becomes white, and white becomes black. Then the layer is ready to be used as a mask.

Creating a mask is normally done by boosting up the contrast a lot, and so forcing pixels in the *hair area* to become *either* back, *or* white. We want the hair to be completely black, and the background to be completely white.

This is best done with Levels. Go to: Colors > Levels. To make the background white, we'll use the *white point picker* (8). Click on the background, and drag. We're looking for a point, where the background becomes as white as possible, while still retaining *as much* hair as possible (9). The trade-off lies in the amount of cleaning up we will have to do afterwards.

Retaining *more hair*, normally has the consequence of having to do *more cleaning up*.

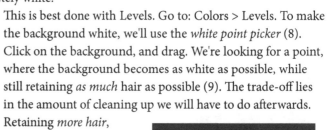

Next select the *black point picker* (10). Click at the top on the hair, and slowly drag to the edge (11). We're trying to find the *optimal* point, where the hair is *best defined*. Then click on OK.

Now that we have defined the blacks and the whites, it's time for the cleaning up. Select the brush. In the *Tool Options* select a brush with 100% hardness. *Alt*-scroll to set the size to 100.

We'll start with filling in the inside of the face, so we paint with black. Paint close, but not too close, along the edge of the hair (12).

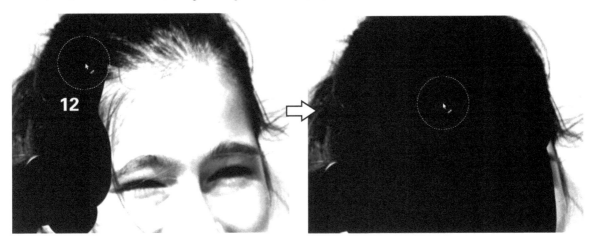

Then zoom in (400%), and with a small *soft* brush, size 20, fill in the edge (13).

If you lower the *Opacity* of the layer (14), you can see the original layer underneath, which helps with filling in the edge (15).

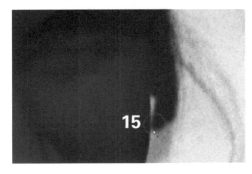

For painting the shoulders, I lower the Opacity even more (to about 30%) to clearly see the edge (16).

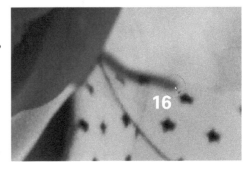

After painting the outline for the shoulders (17), I set the Opacity back to 100%. To fill in the rest of the girl with black (the shirt), I will now use the *free select* tool. I will click *in the middle* of the black line I drew on the shoulders (18).

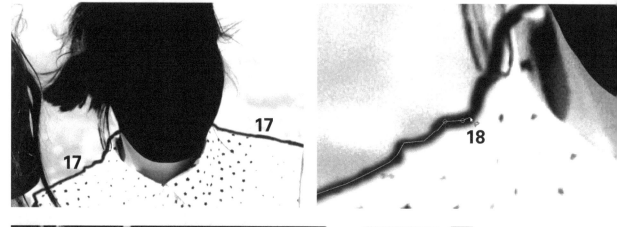

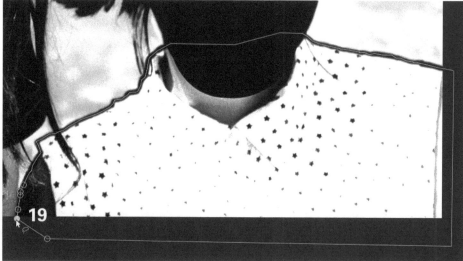

When the selection is ready (19), I fill the selection with black, by pressing *Alt-Backspace*. Press *Ctrl-D* to deselect.

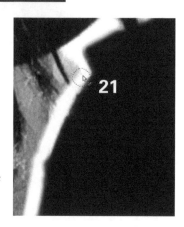

The black part is now ready (20).

The rest will be filled with white. To do this, we'll follow the same procedure. Draw with a small *soft* white brush alongside the finished black border (21), to clear the way for *drawing a selection* in the middle of it again.

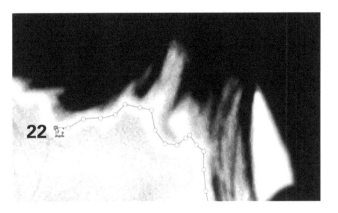

For the outside, I will now use the *Paths* tool (22), which is a bit more flexible than the *Free select* tool.

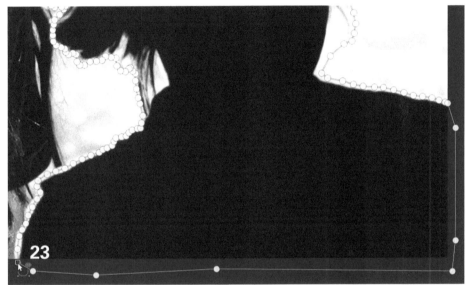

Close the path by *Ctrl*-clicking on the first point (23).

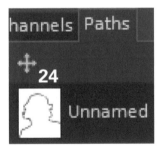

Go to the *Paths* panel (24), and *Alt*-click on the path thumbnail to get a selection from it (25). Press *V* to select the *Move* tool.

At this moment, the *girl* is selected (because I made the path *around* the girl). In order to fill the *background* with white, I have to *invert* the selection.

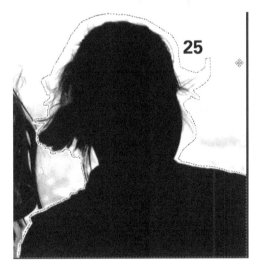

Go to: *Select > Invert* (26). We've turned the selection around. Now I can fill the selection with *white*, by pressing *Alt-Backspace*. Press *Ctrl-D* to deselect (27).

To use this layer as a *mask*, we need to get a *selection* from it. Open the *Channels* panel. The layer we created is black and white, so the *Red*, *Green*, and *Blue* channels will be identical. It doesn't matter which channel we choose to make a selection from. I *right*-click on a Channel and choose: *Channel to Selection* (28). We now have a (Value) selection from our layer. Go back to the *Layers* panel. Right-click on the color layer and choose: *Add layer mask*. Click on *Selection*, and press Enter. Press *Ctrl-D* to deselect.

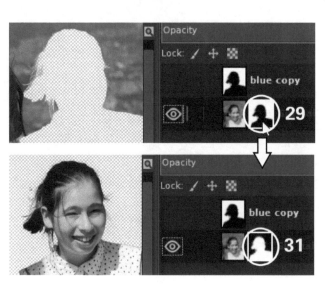

I hide the top layer. We can see I forgot to *invert* my selection (29). The background is now visible, and not the girl. I did this, so I can show you that instead of inverting a *selection*, you can also invert a *layer mask*. With the *mask* selected, go to *Colors > Linear Invert* (30), or press *Ctrl-I*.

We've now *inverted* the mask, and see the girl (31).

Normally, a hair selection will have some *fringing*. *Fringing* means that when the subject that has been cut out, is placed against a *darker* background than it was *originally* in, at some places you will see a light *halo* around the hair. We will now *detect* and *remove* this fringing.

I will place the girl against a *black* background, so *all* existing halo's will become visible. I make a new layer, drag it behind the girl, and fill it with black. Now we can see where the halo's are (32).

Next, we'll remove the fringing by using a *blending mode*. Blending modes are discussed in the next chapter, but I already wanted to show you this trick here.

What the blending mode we're going to use will do, is *hide light* pixels (the fringing) when the image is placed in front of a *dark* background, and *show* the same light pixels, when the image is placed in front of a *light* background. With a light background, you can't see the fringing. And for a natural look, a bit of fringing in a light situation is even welcome. So the blending mode will make the image *adapt* itself to its environment. As a result, the girl can be placed in front of any background.

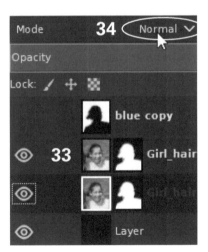

We start with duplicating the color layer (33). Select the bottom color layer. Behind *Mode* (above *Opacity*), we see: *Normal* (34).
If you click on it, you get a list with blending modes. Choose: *Darken only* (35).

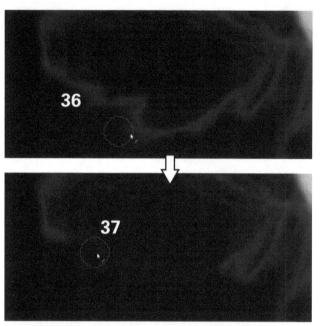

Now select the layer *mask*, of the *top* color layer. Zoom in to about 400%. Here we can clearly see the fringing (36). Select the brush. Choose a soft brush, size 20. Select black (to *hide* pixels). Paint over the halo's you want to remove (37). You can remove the fringing at those places where you think the fringing looks unnatural, when shown in front of a dark background. Some areas (like the top of the head) benefit from a bit softer transition to the background. You can do this by increasing the brush *size*, which will soften the transition.

Now let's have a look at what happens when the background becomes *lighter*. Select the black layer, and open *Levels*.

If you drag the black *Output* slider to the right, you'll see the *hidden* hair slowly *reappears*. To be able to *move* the girl, *link* the two layers so they will move as one (38). How to remove objects like the hair we see on her right shoulder, is discussed in the Retouching chapter.
In the next lesson we will look at cropping an image.

Chapter 4
Cropping, Resizing, and more

33. Cropping

When you're cropping an image you're removing image space that you don't need.
Open *Girl_crop_original.jpg*. Let's say I want to cut out the girl. To do this, select the *Crop* tool (1).

Now drag over the girl (2). The area that will be removed is darkened.

You can adjust the frame, by dragging at the sides and at the corners. You can also *move* the frame by dragging inside the frame. *Clicking once* inside the frame, so without dragging, will *crop* the image. Pressing Enter will also crop the image.

If you have a *specific* size in mind, select *Fixed* in the *Tool Options* (3). Whether you crop for use on *screen*, or whether you crop for *print*, in both cases you will be using *Aspect ratio*.

If you crop for the *screen* (for example for use on the *internet*), it could be that you need a 268 pixels wide, by 421 pixels high image. And in the case of *print*, the destination for your image could be a 4 by 6 inch *photo*. In *both* cases, you're dealing with a *Fixed Aspect ratio* (for *screen*: 268 to 241, for *print*: 4 to 6).

Let's start with the first example. We want an image of 268 pixels wide, and 421 pixels high for use on the internet. Below *Fixed*, we place both numbers, *separated* by a semicolon. So I select the text in the text entry field, and type: 268, a *colon*, and 421 (4).

At the right side you're able to go from *Portrait* to *Landscape*, and the other way around (5). This means if you typed the numbers in the *wrong order*, you *don't* have to *retype* them; just click on the Landscape or Portrait icon, and the numbers are *reversed* automatically!

Now drag over the girl again. The frame you just drew, now has a *fixed* aspect ratio; a *ratio of 268 to 421* (6). You can adjust the *size* of the frame (7), but the *aspect ratio* of the frame (*268* to *421*), *will not change*; because it is fixed.

When you drag the frame to the (bottom) edge, it will *snap* to the edge (like a magnet). Press Enter to crop. The image has now been cropped with the *correct aspect ratio*.

Does this mean my image is now 268 *pixels* wide, and 421 *pixels* high? No, not yet. At the bottom (8) and at the right (9), we see that our image is much *larger*; in my case 1466 pixels wide, and 2303 pixels high. This *is* the correct *aspect ratio*, but we still have *too many pixels* for placement on the internet. So the next step will be to *reduce* the amount of pixels. *Reducing* the amount of pixels of an image is called *resizing*, and this is the topic of the next lesson.

34. Resizing

In the previous lesson, we have cropped an image with an aspect ratio of *268:421*. Now we will look at how to *resize* an image. Go to: *Image > Scale Image* (1). Behind *Width* and *Height*, we see the *pixel* dimensions (2). Our image is 1466 pixels wide, and 2303 pixels tall.

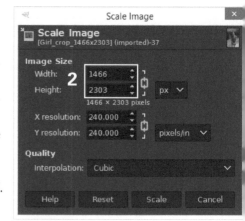

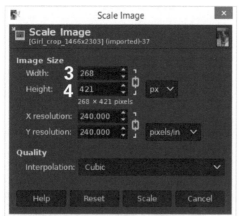

I want to reduce the amount of pixels to 268 pixels for the width, and 421 pixels for the height. So in the *Width* entry field, I type 268 (3). When I press *Enter* (4), I see the *Height* is *automatically* updated and recalculated to 421 pixels. This happens because Width and Height are by default *connected*.

To *disconnect* Width and Height, click on the closed *chain*, which then *opens* (5). I want to leave the image *in proportion*, so I will *close* the chain again, by clicking on the open chain.

Quality is by default on *Cubic*, which gives optimal results (6).

To scale, click on *Scale*. To see the image at 100%, press *Ctrl-1*.
At the bottom we can see we have the correct size: 268 by 421 pixels (7).

We've looked at how to *crop* and *resize* for the web. Now let's look at how to crop for print. After cropping for print, _we don't have to resize_. For print, the resizing is best done by specialised software on the computer that prepares for the printing, and this will go *automatically*. What we *have* to do though, is to *check* whether our image is *large enough* to print. With large I mean large in the *amount* of *pixels*. Not having *enough* pixels, can make your print look *blurry* (or blocky; you will literally start to *see* the square pixels). So it will not print sharp. Let's have a look. I want to crop for a 4 by 6 inch print.

To quickly open one of the ten last opened files, I go to: *File > Open Recent > Girl_crop_original.jpg*.

Select the *Crop* Tool, and in the *Tool Options*, under Fixed, type: 2 : 3 (two colon three), which is the *same* aspect ratio as 4 by 6 (8). Now crop the image.

Next we'll check whether we have *enough* pixels for a sharp print. To make the concept of having *enough* pixels for print *visible*, we will start with using a template. After looking at the template, we will look at how the *Scale Image* window in Gimp gives us the information we need.

For printing *one inch*, we will have to provide *300 pixels*. 300 pixels in a row, *literally* has a 'length' (in *printing terms*) of 1 inch. This means an image of 150x150 pixels, *isn't* large enough to be printed 1 by 1 inch, but can be printed ½ by ½ inch at its maximum. To print *two* inches, we will need at least *600 pixels*, for 3 inches 900 pixels, etcetera. Open *Pixels_to_inches.xcf*. We will now lay this template *over* the cropped image. Drag the *template* thumbnail on the *image* thumbnail (and down a bit so you see a *plus* sign). Then drag the template into place at the top left (it will snap like a magnet). Press *Ctrl-0* to see the whole image. In the template, each inch has a *length* of 300 pixels. Because our image is *larger* than what the template indicates as to be 4 by 6 inches for print (9), we now can *visually* see we have *enough* pixels.

We *don't need* this template however, to check for print. It is just a visual demonstration. In Gimp, the *Scale Image* window will give us the information we need. Go to *Image > Scale Image*. Below *Image Size*, there is *resolution*, which is a *print only* area

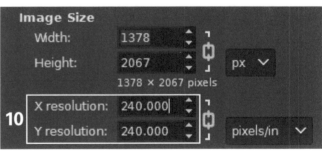

(10). With resolution you *can't* change the amount of pixels. Resolution is just for *calculating* (for checking) whether you have *enough* pixels for print. Select the text behind *X resolution*, type 300 (because 300 is the amount of pixels we need to print 1 inch) and press *Enter* (*Y resolution* is now also 300). Changing the resolution to 300 *didn't* change the *amount* of pixels (11); we still have 1378 by 2067 pixels.

Now that we have set the correct *resolution* for print (300 pixels per inch), at the right of *Image Size* we have to change *pixels* (px) to *inches* (in) (12).

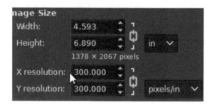

By changing *pixels* to *inches*, Gimp will now divide 1378 by 300, which is 4,593 (*inch* for the Width), and 2067 by 300, which is 6,890 (*inch* for the Height). Although it's a *simple* calculation, it is quite helpful for a quick check! We now know what we wanted to know; we have *enough* pixels to print in the size we have in mind (4x6 inch). We know we can print our image at *4.5 by 6.8* inches at its maximum. Printing smaller is always possible. Printing larger isn't.

Since we haven't changed the pixels, when we *close* the Scale Image window, is there a *difference* between choosing *Scale* and *Cancel* (13)? Yes there is. If we choose *Scale*, the *change* we made in *resolution* (setting it to 300) *is saved*. And this is very useful inside of Gimp. Let me show you. I will make the *rulers* visible via: *View > Show Rulers* (rulers are further discussed in lesson 64; making *e-book* covers). At the bottom left, I will set the rulers to *inches* (14).
Now the *rulers* will tell me the *maximum* size I can print my image (15), (and even more precise than the template did that we had opened).

In the next lesson we will look at how to save images for the web.

35. Save images for the web

In the lecture about cropping, we've *cropped* an image, and *resized* it for use on the internet. In this lecture we'll look at how to *save* an image for the web, and in the next lecture we'll look at how to save an image for print. I have opened 'Save for web'. I go to: *File > Export as*. Behind *Name* (1), you can give your file a different name. Below *Places* (2), you can change the place where you want to

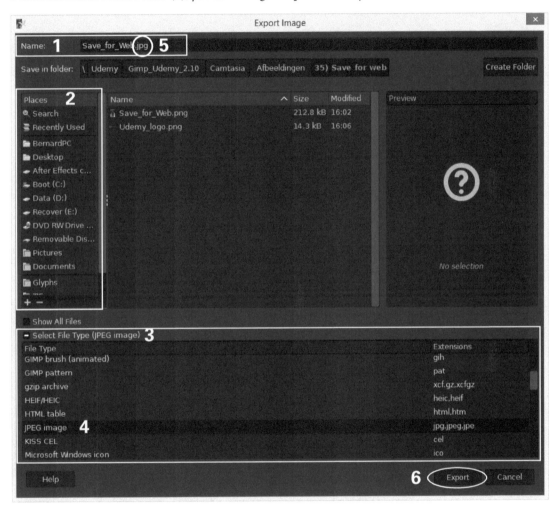

save the file. By default you save in the *same* folder as the image is placed, that you opened. At the bottom left we see: *Select File type* (3). When you click on it, you see a list with different file types. The two most used web file types are JPEG and PNG. Let's have a look at which file type is best suited for which type of image. We'll start with JPEG. I scroll down until I see: *JPEG image* (4). I click on it. At the top we now see our file name ends with *.jpg* (5). Click on *Export* (6).

The *Export Image as JPEG* window opens (7). When you click on: *Show preview in image window* (8), a second (preview) document opens (9). I drag the *Export Image as JPEG* window to the side (10), and zoom in on the image (11) to clearly see the JPEG compression.

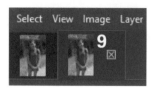

Below in the task bar, I will make the *Export Image as JPEG* window visible again (12).

JPEG's are for photographs. With JPEG's it's best to leave Quality at 100% or close to 100%. This is because jpg uses 'lossy' compression, which means you can damage your image if you compress to much. I zoom in by *Alt-scrolling*. This is what a JPEG looks like if you compress too much (13). I click on the *'Show preview'* button, to compare with, and without compression. So compression with JPEG is a trade-off between File size, shown below the *Quality* slider, and image quality. At maximum Quality, the file size is 153 kB (kilobyte). At Quality 98, we've already lost 50 kB, a third of the size. And if I click on the *Preview* button, I see the compression isn't noticeable. To save the image click on *Export*.

The next format is PNG. Because PNG uses a 'lossless' compression (which means compression *without* losing image quality) PNG is the best choice for saving logo's and icons. First we'll look at what happens when I save our photo in the PNG format. I go to: *File > Export as* again. At the bottom, I scroll down and click on PNG image (14). At the top I see my file name now ends with *.png*. I click on *Export* (15). The *Export Image as PNG* window opens (16). With PNG you can always leave the *Compression level* at 9 (which is the highest compression level) because you *can't* see the compression. Because there is nothing to compare, we don't have a *preview* option as we had with

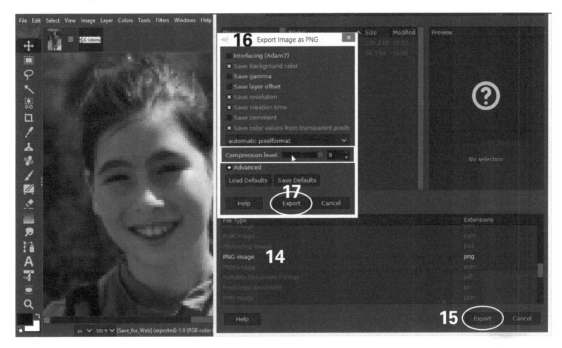

jpg. I click on *Export* (17). At the highest compression level the *png* image is 200 kB, so *twice* the size as the jpg image. When we had compressed the *jpg* image more, the size would have been three or four times larger. This shows that jpg is better suited for photographic images. Now let's look at the *advantages* of png *over* jpg, when saving logos and icons.
Open the Udemy logo. The Udemy logo has transparency; as we can see from the checkerboard pattern. For the internet, this means that *there* where there is transparency, we are able to look *behind* the logo, which is very powerful. JPEG *can't* do this, because JPEG *doesn't* support transparency.

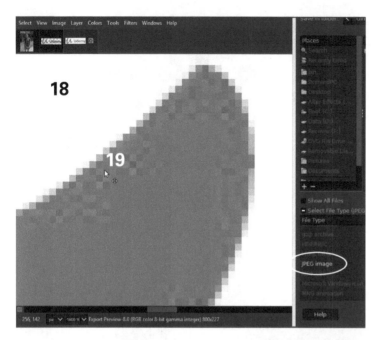

I go to: *File > Export as*. Let's first look at jpg. As soon as I click on the *Preview* button, I see the transparent background is filled in with *white* (18), meaning we *lost* the transparency. Also, JPEG quickly gives artefacts at the edges (19). At *Quality 90*, we already see a lot of jpeg compression. The file size is 21 kilobyte. In the *Export Image as JPEG* window I click on *Cancel*.

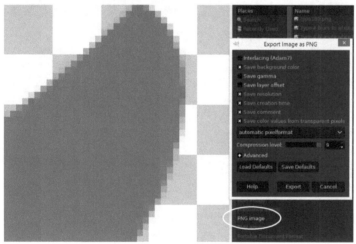

Now let's go to PNG. As we see, with PNG the artefacts are gone, and we have transparency. With JPEG the file size was 21 kb. With PNG the logo is 13 kB, so much smaller!
So PNG not only provides transparency, it also has no artefacts, and for logos and icons, it even gives a smaller file size!

In the next lecture we'll look at how to save for print.

36. Save images for print

If you want a *professional* print of your image, for example printed by
a printing office, or you want to use an image for placement in a magazine,
it's best to save your file in the *tif* file format. Tif stands for: *Tagged Image File
Format*. Tif is sometimes written as *tif*, and sometimes written as *tiff*; both are
the same. Tif is a popular file format in the *graphic design* industry.

To save an image as a *tif*, go to: *File > Export As*. At the top you can give your
file a name. At the bottom left click on *Select File Type* (1). Close to the bottom
you will see: *TIFF image* (2). When you click on it, at the top, you will see your

file name now ends
with *tif*. Under
Places, navigate
to the folder where
you want to save the
file. Click on *Export*,
and then click on
Export again (3).
The file size of a *tif*

file, will be *larger* than that of a JPEG or PNG file.

When an image is going to be printed on paper, the *Red*, *Green*, and *Blue*
color Channels will be translated to a *Cyan*, *Magenta*, *Yellow*,
and *Black* Channel. This conversion is, like the *resizing* of an image
for print, best done by specialized software at the printing office.

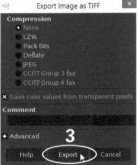

When you send your image for print, it is advisable that you include the
term *sRGB* into your file name. So for example: *'Mountains_sRGB.tif'*.
When information about the *sRGB* color space is missing, normally *sRGB*
is *automatically* assumed. But because there *are more* RGB color spaces, it's
better to include *sRGB* in the file name, so a prepress specialist will know how
to do the conversion correctly.

Gimp *can* do RGB to CMYK conversions, however, this requires *both* an extra
plugin, and *specific* knowledge about color management, which is a relatively
difficult subject. If you're interested in the topic of color management, you can
google for: *Separate+*, which is the *CMYK Separation Plugin* for Gimp.

In the next lesson we will look at transforming layer content.

37. Transformations

Transforming a layer has now become similar to how it works in Photoshop. Not only can you now scale, shear, rotate, and place a layer into perspective, all by pressing *Ctrl-T*, constraining the proportions has moved from the *Ctrl key*, to the *Shift key*, as it is in Photoshop. To *skew* an image, you can drag one of the four white diamonds at a side (1). You can skew in two ways. You can skew *without* the *Shift* key, so without constraining (2). I press *Ctrl-Z* to undo. And you can skew *with* the *Shift* key (3).

To *resize*, you can drag one of the eight squares (4). You can drag, for example from a *side*, *without* the Shift key (5). Or from a *corner*, *with* the Shift key (6), to constrain the proportions.

The corners have a *double* function. If you hold your mouse above the *square*, the square will become *yellow* and you can scale. And if you hold your mouse above the *diamond* (7), the diamond will become *yellow*, and you can place the image in *perspective*.

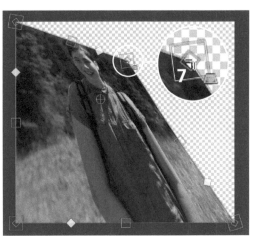

You can *rotate* by holding the cursor *outside* the transformed area, and drag (8). And if you hold the cursor *inside* the transformed area, you can *move it* to another place.

Press *Enter* to apply the transformation. So with the *Unified Transform tool* you can now make multiple transformations *all at the same time*.

Now let's place this image on a computer screen. I Open 'Screen' (9). Here we have a laptop screen that's placed in perspective. The screen has an aspect ratio of *16 by 10*. So I will crop my image in the correct dimensions first, which is 16 by 10. I select *Fixed* (10), and under it, I type: 16:10. Now I drag over my image, position the crop area, and press Enter. I drag

the image over (11). I zoom in on the laptop screen. With the Move Tool I position the top left corner of the image, close to the top left corner of the screen. I press *Ctrl-T* (12).

I will first drag each corner approximately into place. After this I zoom in, and fine-tune the placement of the corners. I press *Enter*. The image has now been placed in perspective on the screen (13).

With the *Unified Transform tool* you can not only transform layers. You can also transform *selections* and *paths*. Let's have a look at an important *difference* between transforming selections and paths. Open 'Selection_vs_path'. On top, we have a text layer (14). The use of *text* is explored further in the next lesson. There are three ways to make the text (the letter a) larger. We can enlarge the letter a just as normal *text*, as a *selection*, and as a *path*. In order to compare transforming *selections* and *paths*, I will first enlarge the letter a as a *selection*, and then enlarge the letter a as a *path*.

Make a selection from the letter a by *Alt-clicking* on the text layer (15). Then press *Ctrl-T*. To scale the *selection*, in the *Tool Options*, behind *Transform*, click on the *Selection icon* (16). Then click on the canvas. Press *Shift* to constrain the proportions, and drag a corner out. Then press *Enter*. I select the *Move* tool, and *Alt-drag* the selection a bit to the right. *Shift-click* on the *New layer* icon, and press *Alt-Backspace* to fill the selection with black. Press *Ctrl-D* to deselect.

As we can see, the enlarged a looks blurry (17)! The reason for this, is that selections are pixel-based. The *solution* for this, is to scale *not* as a selection, but as a *path*.

To do this, *right-click* on the text layer, and choose: *Text to Path* (18). Gimp has now made a *path* of the letter a. Click on the *Paths* panel. We see a path that has been called *'a'* (19). If you make the eye of the path visible (20), on the canvas you will see a *red outline* of the path.

Go to the *Layers* panel, and make a new layer. Press *Ctrl-T*. In the *Tool Options*, behind *Transform*, select the *Path icon* (21). Now click on the canvas. Press *Shift* to constrain the proportions, and drag a corner (or side) out. You can reposition the frame by dragging inside the frame. Press *Enter* to scale. In the *Paths* panel, *Alt-click* on the thumbnail to get a selection from it. Click on the eye to hide the red outline of the path again. Go to the *Layers* panel, and fill the selection with black by pressing *Alt-Backspace*.

We can now see the path gives a very sharp result (22). This is because a path is resolution (and thus pixel) *independent*. No matter the size, a path will always be sharp. This is the reason why logos are normally made in a 'vector' program like Inkscape, where you work only with paths. Inkscape is like Illustrator, and is Open Source, like Gimp.

Selection   Path

Now let's have a look at the Rectangle layer. Hide all the 'a' layers, and make the 'Rectangle' layer visible (29). Let's say we want to make the black rectangle much higher. I *Alt-click* on the Rectangle layer to get a selection of its shape. Then in the *Tool Options*, click on the *Selection icon*, in order to scale the selection. Click on the canvas, and drag the bottom down (29). Press *Enter* to scale. Create a new layer, and fill the selection with black. Press *Ctrl-D* to deselect, and hide the original Rectangle layer.

We can see that the top and bottom (that have been scaled up) have become blurry (30).
The solution for this could be converting to a path again, but there is an *easier* way.

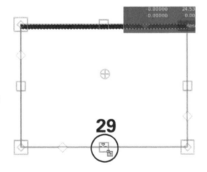

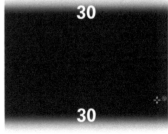

Alt-click on the Rectangle layer again. As we saw in lesson 23, we can make a normal rectangle or ellipse selection *adjustable* again by clicking on it. So to make our rectangle selection adjustable again for use with the *Rectangle select* tool, just click on it *with* the *Rectangle select* tool.

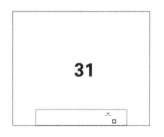

Now I will drag the bottom down again, just like I did with the Scale tool (31). I make a new layer, and fill the selection with black. I press *Ctrl-D* to deselect (32). As we can see, scaling a normal rectangular selection *up*, with the *Rectangle select* tool, *doesn't* give a blurry result, and works fast!

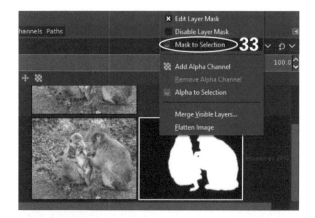

When the selection is more complex than just a simple rectangle or ellipse, you do need to convert to a path before scaling (when the result has to remain sharp). But when the selection comes from a layer *mask* (to do this: *right-click* on the mask, and choose: *Mask to Selection* (33)) and the mask also contains *soft* edges (which normally is the case), you have to scale as a *selection*, in order to keep the softness of the edges.

You can also flip, or, mirror a layer. To do this, go to: *Layer > Transform > Flip Horizontally* (34, 35).

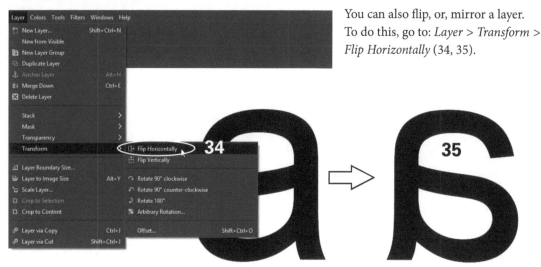

Flipping Vertically is the same as flipping Horizontally, followed by a 180 degree rotation.

If you have an image that's not scanned straight, or you have a picture of a landscape with a skewed horizon, you can use the *Measure* tool to straighten your image. I have opened 'Beach'. I go to: *Tools > Measure* (36). I draw a line across the horizon (37). You can zoom in and adjust the end points if needed (38). In the *Tool Options*, click on *Straighten* (39). By default, this *won't* trim off the corners, that are now *outside* the canvas (40). What I want, is to *rotate* the image, and have the resulting transparency *removed*, without having to use the *Crop* tool. To do this, behind *Clipping* I choose: *Crop to result* (41), before I click on *Straighten* (42). Then I go to: *Image > Crop to Content*, to remove the transparent border (44). We were now able to quickly straighten *and* crop the image.

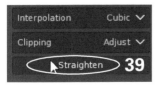

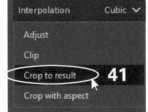

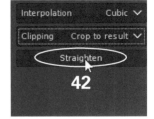

Finally, we will look at the difference between rotating a single *layer*, versus rotating the entire *image*. Open *Canyon_portrait.jpg*. I would like to change this image from *landscape* to *portrait*. To do this, I need to rotate the *image*, and *not* the layer. Let's see what happens if I would rotate the *layer*. Then I would go to: *Layer > Transform > Rotate 90° clockwise* (45).

I have now rotated the *layer*, but *not* the *image* (46). I press *Ctrl-Z* to undo.

To rotate the whole *image*, I must use the *Image* menu (*not* the *Layer* menu). I go to: *Image > Transform > Rotate 90° clockwise* (47).

Now I have rotated the *image*, from landscape to portrait (48).

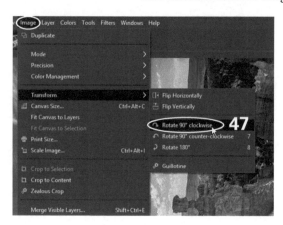

In the next lesson we will look at using text.

38. Using text

In this lecture we will look at the *Text* tool. You can click on the *Text* tool in the *toolbar*, or you can press *T* (1). Now drag a frame on the canvas.

As with the *Rectangle* select tool, you can adjust the *size* of the frame by dragging the sides and the corners (2). The text frame is the *container* or boundary for the text. The text *can't* go outside this frame. This is the way how *Desktop Publishing* programs work.

I will type `Gimp` (3). The default text color will be the Foreground color. To change the text color, go to the

Tool Options, and click behind *Color* on the colored thumbnail (4). I will change the color of the text to a grey, by dragging *Value* to about 60 (5), and press *Enter*. To continue typing, click inside the text frame, to select the frame again. Now I type a space, and the word `text`.

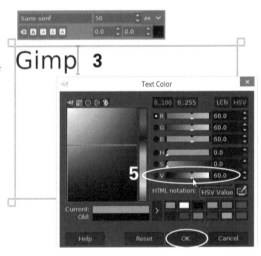

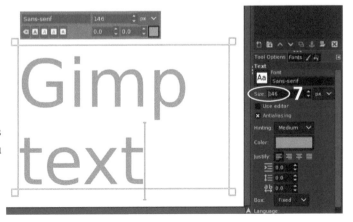

If you hold down the *Alt*-key, the *Move* tool icon will appear (6). So by pressing *Alt*, you can *move* the frame around, by dragging inside the frame.

To change the text size, in the *Tool Options* click behind *Size* in the text entry field, so you get a blinking cursor (7).

With the *up* and *down* arrow keys, it's now easy to adjust the text size. If you keep an arrow key pressed down longer, you go faster.

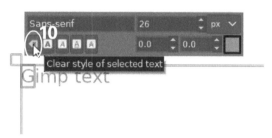

If you want to change the *size* of an *individual* letter, for example you want to make the *G* bigger, use the *small menu* above the text. Select the *G* by dragging over it. In the small menu, click inside the *text size* entry field, to get a blinking cursor (8). With your up and down arrow keys, adjust the size of the *G* (9). Click somewhere in the text box to deselect the *G*. If you now go to the *Tool Options*, you will see that changing the text size from *here*, doesn't affect the *G* anymore. The *G* now can *only* be adjusted with the small menu. If you want the *G* to be a *normal* letter again, select it, and click on the *Clear style of selected text* icon at the left (10). You can now adjust the *G* again with the *Tool Options*.

To explore the text options further, let's insert some placeholder text. Double-click on *Lorem*

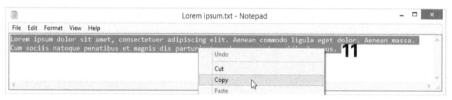

ipsum.txt to open it. Copy the text by pressing *Ctrl-A* to select all the text, and then

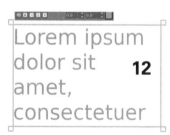

Ctrl-C to copy the text (11). Go to Gimp, and click inside the text frame. To delete the text in the text frame press *Ctrl-A*, and then press *Backspace*. Paste the copied text by pressing *Ctrl-V*. As we can see, there is too much text to fit the frame (12). Let's make the text smaller, and set the size to 20. If you want the text *frame* to be less wide, you can drag the *left or right* side of the text frame in (13). At the bottom you can see the *dimensions* of the text frame (14). I'll drag the *width* of the frame to about 400 pixels (15).

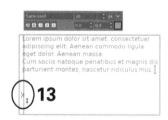

In the *Tool Options* you can align the text. At the right of *Justify* you can choose: *Left* (standard), *Right* (16), *Centered* (17), and *Filled* (18).

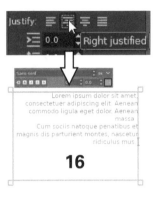
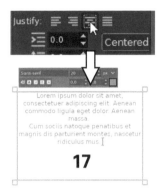
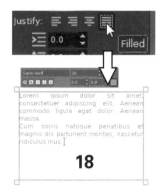

Below *Justify*, you can *indent* the first line of a *new paragraph*. Click in the text entry field, and with your up and down arrow keys you can adjust the distance (19, 20). Below is *line spacing* (21). You can increase or decrease the line spacing (22). Below line spacing is *letter spacing* (23); here you can adjust the space *between* the letters (24).

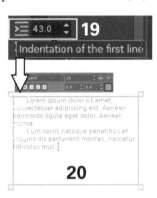
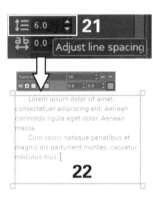

To select a word, you *double-click* on it (25). To select a paragraph, you *triple* click (26). And to select all text in the frame, press *Ctrl-A* (27). Click in the text to deselect.

To break up a word at the end of a sentence, type a *hyphen* inside that word.

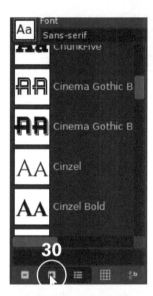

To choose a different font, in the *Tool Options* click on the white font icon (28). You get a list where you can see your fonts. You can quickly scroll through the list by using the scroll bar at the right (29).

You can make the font previews larger and smaller by clicking on the plus and minus magnifying glasses (30).

You can *search* a font by *name*. To do this, select the text under *Font*. Let's say I want to use Arial. If I type the first letter, the letter a (31) (and this *doesn't* have to be a capital letter) I see all fonts that start with an a (32). I can scroll through them.

If I type a second letter, the letter r (33), the list gets *smaller* and shows all fonts that start with ar (34).

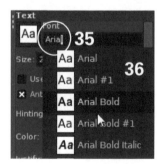

I also type i and a (35), and the Arial font-family remains (36). I have five different font-weights to choose from: Regular, Bold, Bold-italic, Heavy, and Italic.

To experiment with some different fonts, it's convenient to use the *Fonts* panel (37). Click on a font, and by pressing the *up* and *down* arrow keys, you can directly preview new fonts. Holding the up or down arrow key pressed down, let's you go through the list *fast*.

If you don't have the Text *tool* selected, and you're not working on a text *layer*, *double-clicking* on a text *layer* will automatically select the Text *tool* for you! Click inside the text frame and you can type.

You can also *kern* text. *Kerning* is adjusting the space between *two individual letters*. This way, you can position *each letter* exactly where you want. Kerning is used for important and usually *larger* text. For example to make the title of a book cover, or the name of a logo, look more professional or unique. I delete all text in the frame, and type Perfect match as a title. I make the text frame a bit larger, to about 700 pixels wide. In the *Tool Options* I set the letter spacing back to 0. I click inside the *Font size* text entry field, and set the size to about 120.
To improve the text, I think I want to reduce the distance between the P and the e a bit. To do this, I place the cursor between the P and the e (38). In the panel above, at the bottom right, is the *Change kerning* entry field. I click inside the entry field, to get a blinking cursor.

Now I use the up and down arrow keys, to adjust the distance. I think -6 looks good (39).

Because individual letters that are adjusted with the *small* panel (above the text frame), become *unresponsive* to changes in the *Tool Options* panel, and can't be resized anymore via the *Tool Options*, it's best to save specially *kerned* text that you've been working on, as a *path*. This has several advantages. First, you can *scale, rotate, skew,* and place the text in *perspective* (3-dimensionally), *all* without losing *any* sharpness of the text, which is very powerful. Second, you can also *save* the path of the kerned text. When you save a path, you can open the saved path and use it in *other* documents. Let's see how this works. First *right-click* on the text layer, and choose: *Text to Path* (40).

In the *Paths* panel, I now have a path of the *kerned* text (41). To *save* the path, I go to: *Configure this tab > Paths Menu > Export Path* (42).

You can save the path where you want. I will create a *folder* in the *2.10* folder, named: *Paths*, to keep my paths all in one place, so I don't have to search for them.

I call the path `Perfect match`, and click on *Save* (43).

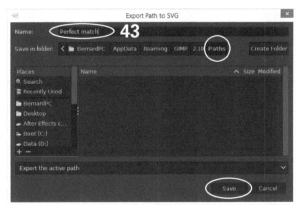

To *open* your path in another file, go to the *Paths* panel. Go to: *Configure this tab > Paths Menu > Import Path.*

At the bottom right, click on *Scalable SVG image*, and choose: *All files* (44). Now select the path you saved (45).

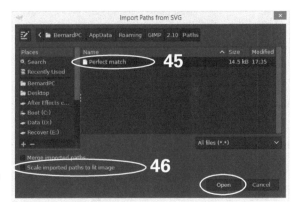

Selecting *Scale imported paths to fit image* is very helpful when the pixel dimensions of your *current* file differs greatly from the one the path was *originally* made in (46). Click on *Open*.

We have now *imported* a path. To see the path as a red outline, make the eye of the path visible. Press *Ctrl-T*. In the *Tool Options*, make sure the *Path icon* is selected. Then click on the canvas. To scale the path proportionally, press *Shift* and drag a corner (or side). You can *move* the path, by dragging inside the Path (47). Then press *Enter*.

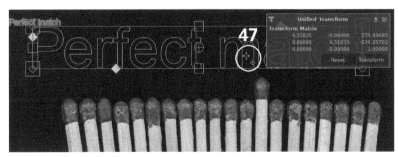

Alt-click on the path thumbnail to get a selection from the path. I create a new layer, I *fill* the selection with white, and deselect (48).

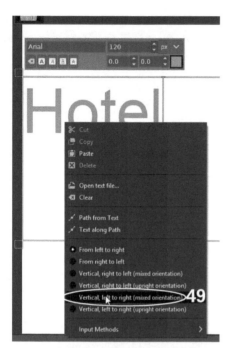

New in Gimp 2.10 is *vertical* editable text. This wasn't possible before. When you rotate a text layer, the text will be rasterized. This means you will lose the ability to *edit* the text (the text will be changed to pixels). Now you can rotate text 90 degrees clockwise, in two different ways.

I will type the word Hotel. To rotate the text, I *right-click* on the text frame, and choose: *Vertical, left to right (mixed orientation)* (49).

This will rotate the text 90 degrees clockwise, and the text is editable (50). I will make the text orange and a bit smaller.

The second vertical text option is: *Vertical, left to right (upright orientation)* (51). Now each letter is shown horizontally, but the letters are placed on top of each other. The two options above do the same as the two options below, but have the *right side* of the frame as the starting point of text.

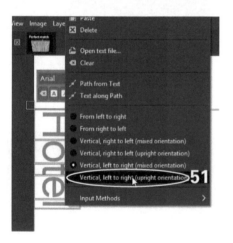

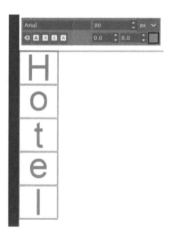

In the next lesson we will look at how to insert special characters, called *glyphs*.

39. Using Glyphs

Most fonts have special characters, often referred to as glyphs. In this lecture we will install a glyphs file, which will serve as a glyphs panel. With the file, you can quickly find a *special* character. Download the file that comes with this lecture, called *Glyphs.xcf*. I will place this file in the *2.10* folder for quick access.

In the *2.10* folder, I will create a new folder called *Glyphs*, and place the *Glyphs.xcf* file in the *Glyphs* folder. In Gimp I go to *File > Open*. I navigate to the *Glyphs* folder in the *2.10* folder, and *bookmark* the *Glyphs* folder. The glyphs file can now be accessed quickly.

Open *Arrow.xcf*. It has a text layer with the text Arrow. If you *double-click* on the text *layer*, the *Text* tool will be selected *automatically*! The font used here is Times New Roman.

Let's say I need a special character for the o. Go to: *File > open*, or press *Ctrl-O*. Click on *Glyphs*, and click on *Open*. To quickly zoom in and make the *Glyphs* document *fill* the window (from *side* to *side*), go to: *View > Zoom > Fill Window* (1).

With the scrollbar at the right, you can quickly scroll through the list of glyphs.

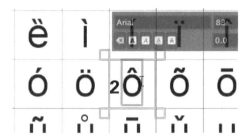

At the top, we have the small and capital letters with diacritical marks. Let's say I need an o with a circumflex. I drag over the glyph (2), and press: *Ctrl-C*. I go back to my Arrow document, drag over the o (3), and press: *Ctrl-V* (4).

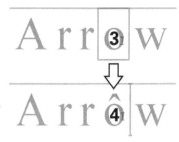

Let's also place a *bullet* point. I click on the Glyphs document, and scroll to the bottom. I drag over the small bullet (5). I *right-* click, and choose: *Copy* (6).

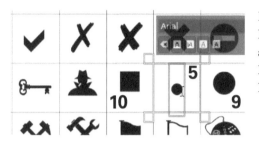

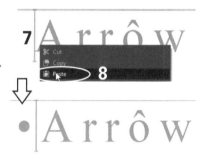

I go back to my Arrow document, and click in front of the A (7). I *right-click*, and choose: *Paste* (8). If you want a larger bullet, you can choose the larger bullet at the right of the small bullet (9). And if you want a square bullet, you can choose the square at the left (10).

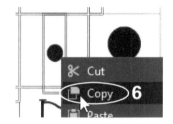

Finally, let's insert an arrow. Scroll to the arrow section. Select an arrow and copy it (11). Go back, click behind the W, and paste the arrow (12).

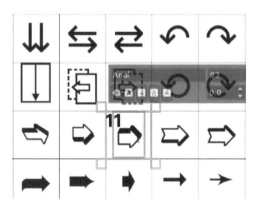

In the next lecture we will look at Blending modes.

40. Blending modes: darken-lighten

In the lecture about selecting hair, we've already seen a blending mode in action. A blending mode will turn a layer onto a *filter*. When you give a layer a blending mode, you will be able to look *through* that layer (in a specific, selective way) *without* lowering the *Opacity* of that layer. So the layer will now to let *some* information through (for example all the light colors from beneath), and at the same time blocks *other* information (for example all the dark colors from beneath). For this reason, blending modes are very powerful, and give results that are not possible to get in another way. Blending modes can roughly be categorized in four groups:

Blending modes that make underlying layers *lighter* (1), blending modes that make underlying layers *darker* (2), blending modes that give underlying layers more *contrast* (3), and blending modes that change the *color* of the layers below (4). In three lectures, the most used blending modes will be discussed. In this lesson we look at *lighten* and *darken* blending modes. In the next lesson we look at *contrast* blending modes. And the *color* blending modes are discussed in the last blending modes lesson.

To see a blending mode in action, you need *two* layers or more. The blending mode will be applied to the *top* layer. The layer or layer's under it, are the ones that the top layer will interact with. Open 'Stars' and 'Mountains'.
The Stars image has *stars* in the sky. I would like to borrow the *stars* from the Stars image and *place* them in the sky of the Mountains image. Drag the Stars image over to the Mountains image (6). Go to *Mode*, and choose the *Lighten only* blending mode (7). Now we have stars in the sky (8).

So how does *Lighten only* work? What the *Lighten only* blending mode does is it makes a *comparison*: which layer has the *lightest color*? Is it the layer with the blending mode, or any of the layers below it? For each pixel, this comparison is made. The lightest pixel wins, and will be shown.

I just want the stars, and not the light mountains that have become visible at the bottom (9). So I will *remove* the light mountains using a layer *mask*. *Right*-click on the top layer and choose *Add Layer mask*. Choose a white mask, and press Enter. To hide the mountains, paint with black. Press *B* to select the brush, and in the *Tool Options* choose a hard brush. Increase the size to about 400. After painting away the light mountains *only* the stars will now come through (10). You can lower the *Opacity* of the *Stars* layer a bit to get a more subtle effect.

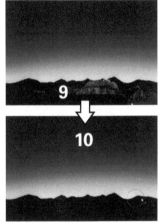

Next we'll look at the *opposite* of *Lighten only*: *Darken only*. We've already seen this blending mode in action in lesson 32 about selecting hair. Let's explore *Darken only* a bit further. Open 'Amsterdam', 'Clouds', and 'Birds'. I would like to place some clouds in the sky. Drag the 'Clouds' image over to the 'Amsterdam' image (11). Go to *Mode*, and choose *Darken only* (12).

With *Darken only*, only the *darkest* pixels will be shown. That's why we see the clouds; the Clouds are *darker* than the very bright sky (13). Below the sky, we see the buildings, because the buildings are *darker* than the clouds.

Let's optimize the result a bit. To prevent that the clouds will interact with the buildings, I make a selection of the cloudless sky in the Amsterdam layer. To do this, click in the *lightest* area of the sky with the *Fuzzy* select tool, and drag the *Threshold* to about 120 (14).

With the selection loaded, *right*-click on the *Clouds* layer, and choose: *Add Layer Mask*. Click on *Selection*, and press *Enter*. Press *Ctrl-D* to deselect. I still see a bit of *white* from the *old* sky inside some trees (15). To *reveal* the

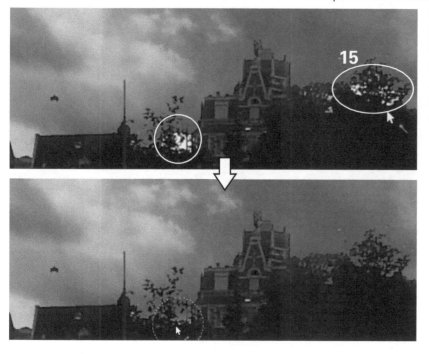

new sky in the trees, press *B* to select the brush and set the size to about 60. Paint with *white* in the layer *mask* to reveal the new sky.

I want to create a *new* layer from what I see now, like a *snapshot*. To do this, *right-click* on the top layer, and choose: *New from visible* (16). I have now added a *flattened* version of my document, in *one* layer.

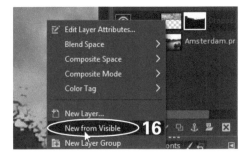

I will now *brighten* this new layer. Press *Ctrl-L* to open *Levels*, and drag the middle slider to the left.

I also would like to put some birds in the sky. Open 'Birds'. Drag the birds over (17). I want to see the birds, but *hide* it's grey background to see the clouds underneath. I will start by setting the birds layer to *Darken only* (18).

Because almost *everything* on the Birds layer is *darker* than the sky underneath, almost the complete *Birds* layer stays visible (19).

To change this, I will open *Levels*. I will brighten the image with the midtone slider, until the background of the birds gets *lighter* than the sky under it (20). Now *only* the birds are darker than the background (21).

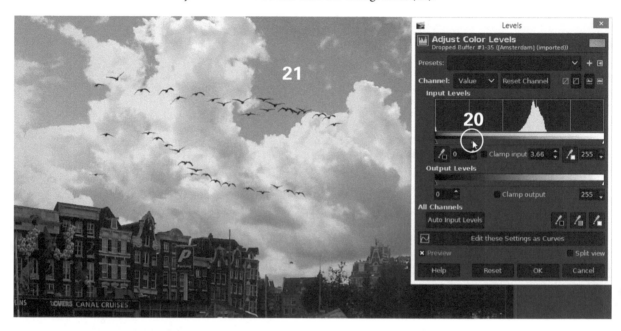

Next we will look at *Screen* and *Multiply*. Like *Lighten only* and *Darken only*, *Screen* and *Multiply* are *opposites*.
Open 'Mountains' and 'Girl_crop'. Drag the girl image over.

I place the girl layer partially over the dark mountains. When I set the girl layer on *Lighten only*, I will see only the *lightest* pixels (22). This means only *part* of the girl, and only a *part* of the Mountains. But what if I want to see both images completely? Below *Lighten only*, select *Screen*.

Screen can be compared to using *two separate slide projectors*, who are both projecting on the *same* screen. One projector shows the mountains, the other projector shows the girl. Where the two images overlap, we get a *slightly lighter* result (23), but *both* images *will* be visible, which is what we want.

Open *Lens_flare.jpg*. I would like to *add* this lens flare to the girl image, to give it a sunny effect. I drag it over.

For adding the stars, we used *Lighten only*. If we use *Lighten only* for the lens flare however, we're not getting the result we are looking for. There is no real blending going on (24). The only way to add the *actual light* from the flare, is to use the double slide projector technique provided by *Screen* mode (25).

Screen can also be used to lighten an image *itself*. I hide the flare, and make a duplicate of the girl layer (26). I set the duplicate on *Screen* (27).

With *Opacity* I can adjust the *amount of light* coming from the 'second projector' (28).

You can also *colorize* an image with *Screen*, to bring a certain mood to an image. To warm the image up, I could fill a new layer with orange. Then I set the layer to *Screen*, and drag the *Opacity* down (to about 10 percent). With *Hue-Saturation* I could adjust the *tint* of the orange (by using the Hue slider), to experiment with different colors.

You can also *paint* with colored light, using a soft brush. You could make different layers, each layer having a specific color. When you give these layers a black layer *mask*, you can *add* and *remove* colored light from each layer. When you set the brush *Opacity* low (10%), you can gradually add and remove colored light. Press *X*, to alternate between painting with black and white.

The *opposite* of *Screen* is *Multiply*. For *Screen*, we had the comparison of having *two* projectors, each showing an image. With *Multiply* we're back to *one* projector, showing *both* images at the *same time*. You can compare it to a *light table*, where you lay two transparent sheets on top of each other. The second sheet will make the result *darker*. Open 'Rails'.

Let's say I want an orange circle, and I want to be able to see the background *through* the orange circle. For this, we'll need the *light table* effect. Create a new layer. To draw a circle, select the *Ellipse* select tool. Start dragging, and then add the *Shift* key. To position the circle, drag in the middle of the circle. Now open the color panel, and select an orange.

On an empty layer, fill the selection by pressing *Alt-Backspace*. Press *Ctrl-D* to deselect. Now choose *Multiply* (29).

Below *Multiply* we have *Burn*. Open 'Building'. *Burn* is a variation of *Multiply*, and gives a more dramatic effect. It brings more contrast and saturation, providing a *cinematic* look.

41. Blending modes: contrast

In this lesson we'll look at the *contrast* blending modes. Open 'Plaster'. Let's say I want to mix the plaster and the underlying image. With *Screen* (the two projector method) the result becomes too *light*. And with *Multiply* (the light table method) the result becomes too *dark*. The solution for this is *Overlay* (1). *Overlay* is a *combination* of *Screen* and *Multiply*. *Overlay* will make the light tones lighter, and the dark tones darker, increasing *contrast*.

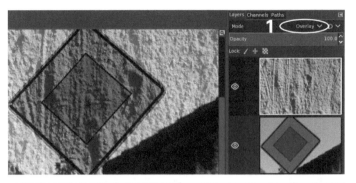

A more extreme version of *Overlay* is *Hard light* (2). Like we saw with *Burn*; *Hard light* gives more *contrast* and more *saturation*.

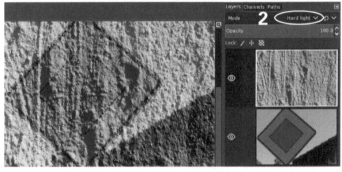

You can also *combine* blending modes. Set the *wrinkled paper* layer to *Overlay*. To make the effect *stronger*, I duplicate the layer. Now the result is getting too *light*. The solution is to change the top layer to *Multiply* (3), to get the desired result. You can lower the *Opacity* to reduce the strength. We now have *Overlay* and *Multiply* working *together*.

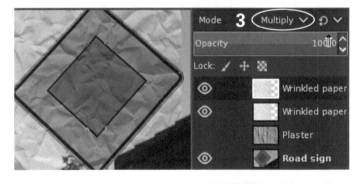

All blending modes in the contrast group (4) are a combination of *Screen* and *Multiply*, except *Vivid Light* and *Linear Light*. They are a combination of *Dodge* and *Burn*.

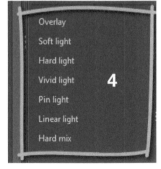

Open 'Contrast_blending_modes'. Here we see six identical gradients going from black to white. They look different however because each gradient has been set to a different *contrast* mode. They are placed in the order from producing mild to the strongest contrast.

We can see the result of *Soft Light* (5) is less strong than that of *Overlay* (6). *Soft Light* has the effect of shining a soft spotlight on the layers below. We can see *Overlay* is able to produce *black* in the layers below, which *Soft Light* isn't. However, *Overlay* is still quite soft in the light colors.
Hard Light (7) is able to produce white, and for this reason will give more contrast than *Overlay*. In a moment we will look at actual image examples of these lighten modes.
Pin Light (8) is different than the other light modes, in that the midtones aren't visible. So only the dark and light colors will blend.

Pin light is very useful in combination with Flare Gradients. Gradients are described in detail in Lecture 44. With the *Gradient* tool selected, I select a Flare glow, and set the layer on *Pin light*. I drag and reposition the gradient (9).
Vivid Light is a combination of Dodge and Burn, so *Vivid Light* will give more contrast and saturation than *Hard Light*, as we can see (10).

And lastly we have *Linear Light* (11), which, of the light modes, has the *strongest* effect on images. As a gradient *Vivid* and *Linear Light* look very similar (10, 11), so now let's look at some actual examples. I open 'Girl_contrast_modes'. With *Vivid* and *Linear Light* you can add powerful light effects to an image. Let's see how they differ. On top we have *Vivid Light* (12), and below *Linear Light* (13) assigned to the same abstract layer. We see *Linear Light* has an even *stronger light effect* than *Vivid Light*.

We'll have a look at the *contrast* modes for *coloring* an image, for special *effects*, and for creating *highlights*. For the blending, I used colored gradients (14). We've already seen *Pin light* with the flare. Here *Pin light* is used to create a lomo color effect (15).

In comparison to *Pin light*, *Hard light* (16) gives a more overall blending, having a different effect.

We've already used *Vivid light* with a warm color, here it is used with a cool color (17).

Soft light (18) is good for warming up an image, without being *overpowering*.

Here *Linear light* is used to *colorize* skin. The blending mode layer has been set

to a lower *Opacity*. Now let's look at some creative uses. Here the face is now visible *inside* the circles (19).

And here we get a *digitalized effect* (20).

You can also produce a *grainy effect*, like an old photo.

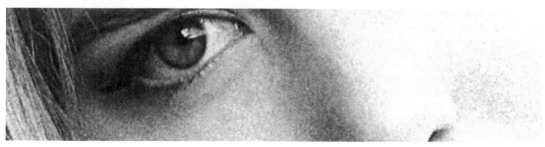

And here the image looks like it is *painted*.

You can use *Vivid* and *Linear Light* to determine the *direction of light* (21). Here we see the light direction is from the *right*. And now the light is coming from the *left* (22).

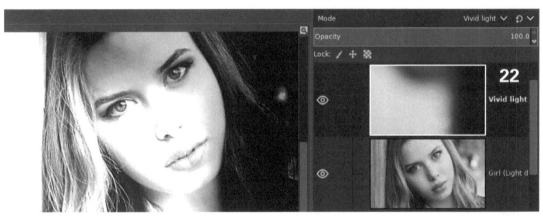

As we see, the *newly* added *contrast* blending modes in Gimp 2.10 are powerful for manipulation color and light, but they can do more. In Gimp 2.10, we're now able to use a professional *sharpening* technique, which is often used in Photoshop. Open 'Girl_portrait'. I would like to make this image sharper. I start with duplicating the layer.

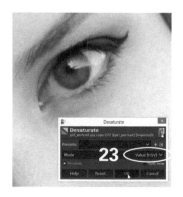

I will zoom in on the girls eye. The *duplicated* layer will be used to sharpen the layer below. I will make the duplicate layer black and white, by going to: *Colors > Desaturate > Desaturate*, or you can press *Shift-Ctrl-U*. I hold my mouse above *Luminance* and scroll with my mouse to compare the different desaturation methods. I think *Value* gives the best definition of the eye (23). I click on *OK*.

Gimp 2.10 now also has a *High Pass* filter, like Photoshop has. I go to: *Filters > Enhance > High Pass* (24). The *High Pass* filter will detect *edges*. I set the black and white layer to one of the *contrast enhancing* blend modes. I will start with *Overlay*. By clicking on the *eye* of the *black and white layer*, I can compare the before (25) and after (26). As we can see, the eye has become sharper. I will scroll through the contrast modes to compare the different sharpening results. I see *Linear Light*, for this image, gives the best sharpening, in combination with the *High Pass* filter. I will keep both *Standard deviation* and *Contrast* low, and focus on getting a natural result. When this step is finished, I will further increase the sharpening, by *duplicating* the High Pass *layer* one or more times, when needed, which gives the most *natural* result. I will lower *Contrast* a bit to point 5 (27). I now duplicate the High Pass *layer* (28), and see I get a natural sharpening effect. When I duplicate again, I see the sharpening gets to strong. I can reduce the strength of the sharpening, by lowering the *Opacity* of the layer. I *Shift-click* on the original layer, to see the before and after.

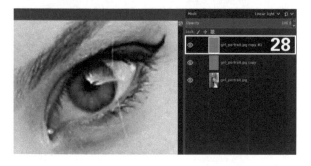

I think the sharpening of the eyes is ok, but I don't want the *skin* sharpened. I *right-click* on the top layer and choose: *New from Visible*. I hide the sharpening layers. I *right-click* on the top layer and choose: *Add Layer Mask*. I choose black, and press *Enter*. I select the *Paintbrush*, and set the size to 50. I paint with a white, soft brush. I paint over the eyes, and the eyebrows. I can paint back the edges where I

accidentally revealed the skin, by painting with black. I will also reveal the mouth, and the bottom of the nose. I will make the brush bigger, and also reveal the hair. I click on the eye of the top layer, to compare the before and after (29). I *right-click* on the top layer again and choose: *New from Visible*, to get the final version.

Gimp and Photoshop both have a sharpening filter, called Sharpen or: *Unsharp mask*, which we will look at in lecture 43. Sharpening with *High Pass* however, is preferred by professionals over *Unsharp mask*, because it gives more *natural* results. To make this visible this, open 'Girl_eye'. I zoom in quite a bit. *High Pass* (left) gives more natural edges, as we can see at the edge of the iris (30).

In 'skin_edge', we see the edge of an arm. The left layer has *High Pass* sharpening applied to it. When I sharpen with *Unsharp mask* (31), I am not able to get the same sharpening result as I get with *High Pass*. The pixels are getting too dark to fast. And there are *color problems*.

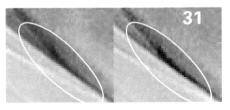

To conclude, thanks to the new *High Pass* filter and *new* contrast blend modes, in Gimp 2.10 we're now able to use a professional sharpening technique. The last contrast mode of the list, *Hard Mix*, is discussed in Lecture 46, where we make duotone images.

42. Blending modes: color

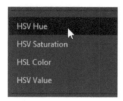

In the third blending modes lesson we'll look at the color group: *Hue*, *Saturation*, *Color*, and *Value*. *Color* is the combination of *Hue* and *Saturation*. The *Hue* blending mode is often used when a *Value* adjustment (with *Levels* or *Curves*) comes with an undesired side effect concerning the color. Open 'Canyon'. Open *Levels*. The more you make the midtones darker, the more you can see the *orange* sand is shifting to *red* sand. If you only want the sand to be darker, and *not* also to become more red, you use the *HSV Hue* blending mode. Before using *Levels*, first duplicate the layer. Set the blending mode of the top layer to *HSV Hue* (1). This layer will now function as a filter, and will *only* let the *Value* changes come through. Click on the bottom layer, and open *Levels*. If you now make the midtones darker, you will see *no* color change! Click on *OK*. If you hide the blending mode layer, you can see the difference between using the Hue 'filter', and without using this filter.

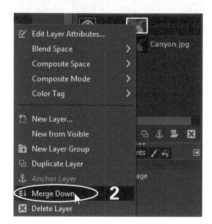

If you want to, you can *merge* the two layers *together* (making them a *single* layer). You do this by *right-clicking* on the top layer, and choose *Merge Down* (2, 3).

I undo the merging by pressing *Ctrl-Z*. You can also keep the layers separated, and put them in a *folder*.
Click on the *Create a new layer group* icon (4, 5).

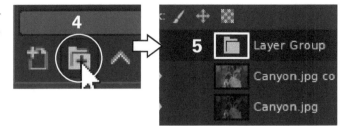

Drag the layers in the *Layer Group* folder (6, 7, 8).

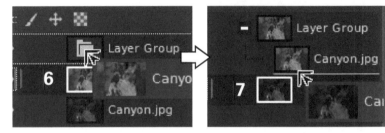

To *close* the folder, click on the *minus* sign in front of the folder.
Now it is just like having *one* layer (9).

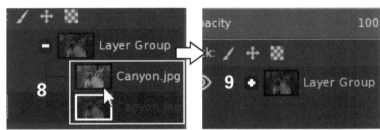

When you *select* the Layer Group *thumbnail*, you can *move* and even *scale* the Layer Group, as it is *one* layer. If you *scale* the Layer Group, *all* layers that are inside the Layer group scale with it (10)!

You can *also* adjust each layer inside the Layer Group *individually*.

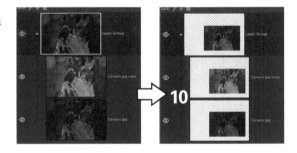

Now let's look at *Color*. Open 'Girl_crop'. Create a new empty layer and set it on *HSL Color* (11). Open the color window, and choose 100% green.

Select the brush. Where you paint over the blue shirt (12, 13) the shirt will now become green. The *Value* of the bottom layer will come through. *Hue* (and *Saturation*) come from the *top* layer. Because the buttons of the shirt also have become green now, you can hide them again by using a layer *mask* for the top layer. Paint with black over the buttons, inside the *mask*.

The last blending mode is *Value*. Open 'Color_cast'. Open the *Channels* panel. We can see that the *Red* channel (14) is *lighter* than the *Green* and *Blue* channels. This is the main reason for the red color cast. So making the Red channel *darker*, will remove the red color cast.

Open *Levels*. Go to the *Red* channel, and make it darker. Although we have lost the color cast, we *also* made the image *darker*. If you want to do a color correction, *without* colors becoming lighter or darker, use the *Value* blending mode.

Go to the *Layers* panel and duplicate the layer. Set the blending mode to *Value*. Select the bottom layer. Open *Levels* and go to the *Red* channel again. If you now drag the slider, you see you're losing the red, but the image *doesn't* become darker.

In the next lesson we will look at methods for blurring.

43. Methods for blurring

Blurring is used for many things. It can be used to create depth of field, for retouching, vignetting, text effects, and for creating drop shadows.

Alternative ways for blurring are motion blur and Bokeh, which

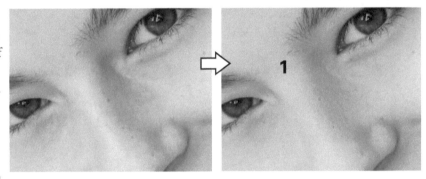

will be discussed in the *Nik collection* chapter, as well as vignette blurring. Blurring for skin retouching (1), called *frequency separation*, is discussed in the Retouching chapter.

In this lesson we will create a drop shadow, a glow, a text fading effect, and depth of field. We will also look at the *Smudge* tool, with which you can smear pixels like wet paint.

We'll start making a drop shadow. Create a new document, and make it 600 by 300 pixels. Click on the Foreground color, and make a grey by dragging *Value* to about 75. Then click on the Background color, and make a lighter grey. Click on OK. Fill the layer with the Foreground color by pressing *Alt-Backspace* (2).

Create a new layer, and call it paper (3). Press *M* to select the *Rectangle* tool. Drag a rectangle, and press *Ctrl-Backspace* to fill it with the Background color (4). Press *Ctrl-D* to deselect.

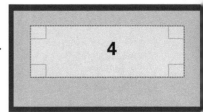

Create a new layer for the shadow, and drag it below the paper layer. Call it shadow (5).

Alt-click on the paper layer to get a selection from it. Click with the *Rectangle* tool *inside* the selection, to make it adjustable. Drag the sides a bit in (6).

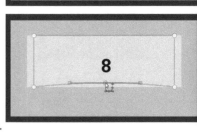

Go to *Paths*, and click on the *Selection to Path* thumbnail (7). Press *Ctrl-D* to deselect, and double-click on the path thumbnail. Press *Ctrl*, and *add* a point in the middle at the bottom. Drag the added point up a bit (8). You can also use your *arrow* keys, to move the point.

Go to *Paths*, and click on the *Selection to Path* thumbnail. Press *Ctrl-D* to deselect, and double-click on the path thumbnail. Press *Ctrl*, and *add* a point in the middle at the bottom. Drag the added point up a bit (8). You can also use your *arrow* keys, to move the point.

Alt-click on the path *thumbnail* to get a selection, and press *V* to select the *Move* tool. Press *D* to set the Foreground to black, and, with the shadow layer selected, press *Alt-Backspace* to fill the selection with black. Press *Ctrl-D* to deselect. Drag the shadow down a bit (9).

Now we will blur the shadow. I go to: *Filters > Blur > Gaussian Blur*. I set *Size* to about 3.5, by dragging the *Size X* or *Y* slider (10). I click on OK.

Select the *Move* tool, and click once on the canvas. Now with your arrow keys, you can fine-tune the position of the shadow (11).

You can drag the *Opacity* of the shadow layer down a bit (12).

Now we'll make a glow. Press *D* to set the Fore- and Background to black and white. Open the Color window, and make a light blue (13). Click on OK. *Shift*-click on the new layer icon. Drag the Foreground color on the canvas. Press *X* to switch the Fore- and Background color. Open the *Glyphs* panel, by going to: *File > Open > Glyphs*. Click on Open. Zoom in a bit and look for the cloud with the sun behind it. Press *T* to select the *Text* tool. Drag over the icon, *right*-click, and choose *Copy* (14). Go to the glow document, click on the canvas, and press *Ctrl-V*. In the *Tool Options*, click on the text *Color* square, select white, and click on OK. Click in the *Font size* text entry field. Hold the arrow up key pressed down until size 300. Press *Alt* and drag *inside* the text frame (15)

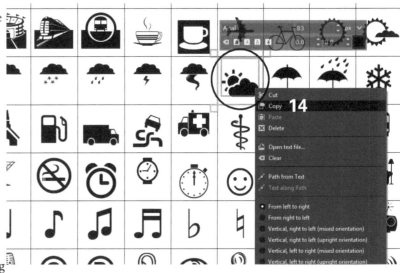

to position the cloud. In the *Tool Options*, click on the text *Color* square again, to open the *Text Color* window. In this window, click on the *eyedropper* at the right, and click in the image on the *blue*, to make the cloud also blue (now everything is blue). Click on OK. Select the blue layer, and *Shift*-click on the new layer icon. *Alt*-click on the text layer to get a selection from it. Go to: *Select > Grow*. I will grow my selection with 20 pixels (16). Click on OK (17).

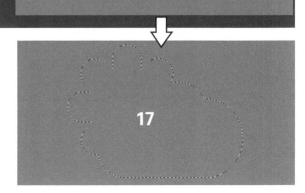

Drag the Foreground color on the canvas (as an alternative for *Alt-Backspace*) (18).
Press *Ctrl-D* to deselect.

Because we have just used Gaussian Blur, you can go to: *Filters > Re-Show "Gaussian Blur"* (19). Adjust the *Blur Size*. Click on *OK* (20).

We can also use Gaussian Blur in just *one direction* (horizontal or vertical), for example to give text a *faded effect*. Open *The man on the train.xcf*. Press *Ctrl-1* to get a 100% view. Duplicate the text layer twice. Select the middle text layer. Go to: *Filters > Re-Show "Gaussian Blur"*. I only want to blur horizontally.

To do this, click on the *chain* icon, to *disconnect* equal blurring (21).

Set *Size X* to about 70 (22, 23). Set *Size Y* to 0. Click on *OK*.

Next select the *bottom* text layer. Go to: *Filters > Re-Show "Gaussian Blur"*. Set *Size X* to about 5 (24, 25), and *Y* to 0. Click on *OK*. Now the text has a bit of extra glow to it. You can adjust the strength of the glow by lowering the *Opacity*.

We will look at more effects for text in the *Google Nik collection* chapter. Now let's look at *depth of field*, which is another use of blur. Open 'Wood'. I would like to create some depth of field at the right,

to direct the viewers eye to the left. Select the *Blur / Sharpen* tool by going to: Tools > Paint Tools > *Blur / Sharpen* (26). In the *Tool Options*, by default, *Blur* is selected (27). If you click on *Sharpen*, the tool will do the *opposite* of blurring: it will sharpen.

Rate determines the *strength* of the blurring or sharpening (28). I set it to 100%.

I will work with a large, soft brush. I set the size to about 800, so the brush *covers* the area I want to adjust. I drag a couple of times from the top to the bottom. Now we see the sharpness slowly fades at the right, introducing a bit *depth* to the image (29).

Now let's look at another blur tool; the *Smudge* tool (30).

With the *Smudge* tool you can smear pixels like wet paint (31).

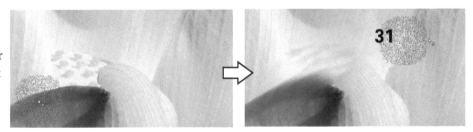

Open 'Old_man'. I used the *Smudge* tool here, to create a painted effect (32). Different brushes with the Smudge tool can give different results.

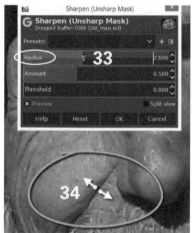

To prepare for getting a painted effect with the *Smudge* tool, I first *sharpened* the image quite a bit, to get strong contours. To do this, go to: *Filters > Enhance > Unsharp mask*.

What *Unsharp Mask* does, is it is looking at the *edges* in an image, and it will increase the *contrast of these edges*. With *Radius* (33) you set how *many* pixels, at the *left* and *right* side of an edge, are given more contrast (33). So you determine the *width* of the edge, that is given more contrast. This means that if you want to sharpen the *finer detail* in an image, you have to set the *Radius* smaller, and if you if you want to sharpen the *larger details*, you have to set the *Radius* larger.

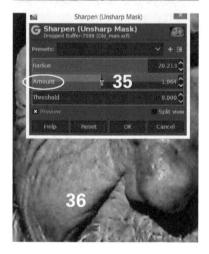

With *Amount* (35) you determine *how strong* the contrast will be. Dragging the slider to the right will *increase* the contrast (36).

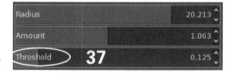

Threshold (37) protects edges with lower contrast, so it *excludes areas* with *less contrast* from being sharpened. The higher the *Threshold*, the more edges that are *not* being sharpened.

For my paint effect, I will increase the *Radius* to 20, which will amplify the *larger* details and lines of the face. I set *Amount* to 1,25.

Now select the *Smudge* tool. To create a *paint* effect, I will use a brush with fine detail. I select *Grass* (38).

For the *Smudge* tool it is important, that the *Spacing* is set to 1. In the *Brushes panel* at the bottom, I drag the *Spacing* slider to the left (39).

In the *Tool Options*, *Rate* determines how *far* the pixels can be *dragged out*, or how 'wet' the paint is (40).

When I set *Rate* higher, for example at 86% (100% is *infinite* repetition), I can drag pixels *further* out, than when *Rate* is set lower, for example at 50%.
I will set *Rate* to 70% for the paint effect.

I will use a soft brush, and set the brush size to 20.
With the *Grass* brush, I paint in the same direction that the lines are going.

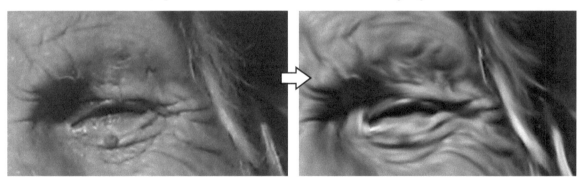

In the next lesson we will look at how to make gradients.

44. Making gradients

A gradient is a color transition from one color to another color. To create a gradient, you use the *Gradient* tool (1). I select it. If I now drag over the canvas, I see I get a gradient from the *Foreground* color to the *Background* color. The transition is between the *Start point* and the *End point* (2).

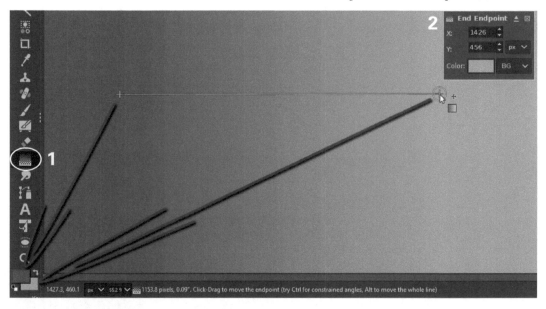

You can drag the *Start* and *End* points to a different location. To get a perfect horizontal or vertical gradient, hold down the *Ctrl* key when you drag a point. To apply the gradient press *Enter*. I press *Ctrl-Z* to undo, and drag again. Now let's adjust the *colors* of the gradient. I click on the *Start* point (3). The *Start* point is connected to the *Foreground* color, as we can see here (4). I click on the *Foreground* color and change it to red. And to change the color of the *End* point, I click on the *Background* color and change it to yellow (5). Now the gradient goes from red to yellow.

You can add additional colors to the gradient, by simply clicking on the line (6). I see my new color has the shape of a diamond, and it has been named: *Stop 1*. By default a new Stop gets the same color that the gradient is showing at the place where you click.

We now see, that a color Stop can be divided in two colors by clicking on the *link icon* (7), which will unlink the *Left* and *Right* color. Before we look at this option (I will link them again) let's give *Stop 1* a new color. I click on the *Left* or *Right* color icon, this doesn't matter because they are linked. I will make a muted blue (0,50,50). I can *drag* the color stop to another place. But I can also position the stop numerically, behind *Position*, for example at a third of the gradient (8).

When I move my mouse to the left, or to the right, I see also two circles on the line (9). Let's click on a circle (10). The circles are the *Midpoints*, called *Midpoint 1* (9) and *Midpoint 2* (10). A Midpoint regulates the *transition* between two colors. You can drag a *Midpoint*, or circle, to the left and the right. By default they are in the *middle* of two colors, but you can change their position.

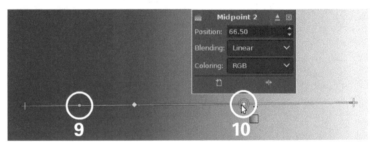

To place the Midpoint in the *middle* again, click on the *Center midpoint* icon (11).

If you *double-click* on a Midpoint, it becomes a new color *Stop*. And when this happens, *new* Midpoints are automatically created.

You can *remove* color Stops by dragging them off the line. When you see a *little minus sign* (12), you can release the mouse.

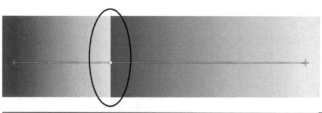

Now let's look at *splitting* a Stop. When I unlink *Left* and *Right* color, I can give the Left and Right color a *different* color, effectively creating *two* gradients inside my gradient.

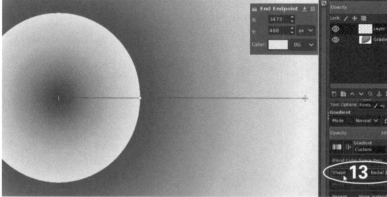

In the *Tool Options* we can change the *Shape* of the gradient. By default we have a *Linear* gradient. When I choose *Radial* (13), the gradient becomes *circular*. I will *delete* the color Stop (*Stop 1*). The Foreground color is now the center, which radiates out to the Background color (14). I can turn this around by pressing the *X* key (15). I press Enter to apply the gradient.

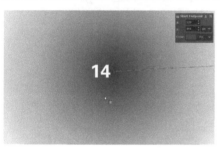

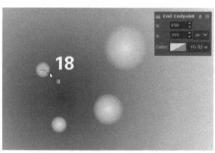

I would like to add some more yellow circles. I do this by having the *Foreground* set to yellow. Then, in the *Tool Options* I click on the color thumbnail (16), and choose: *FG to Transparency* (17). I can now *add* circles (18).

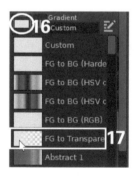

And when I set *Radial* back to *Linear*, I can also add yellow *linear* gradients (19). As we see (16), Gimp has several presets. Most of them have more than two colors, and some of them use transparency. Let's try: Tube Red (20). And in lecture 41 we've already looked at creating flares (21).

A gradient is often used for *blending* images. Open 'Valley_gradient'. I will blend the two images together. I press the *D* key to set the Fore- and Background color to *black* and *white*. And in the *Tool Options* I choose: *FG to BG (RGB)* (22). I set *Shape* to *Linear*. I select the 'wave' layer (23), and click on the: *Add a Mask* icon (24). I choose *Black*, and press *Enter*.

I can now blend the images by using a gradient.

I can also try a *Radial* gradient, and I can also adjust the *Midpoint* to regulate the transition (25).

In the next lecture we'll look at patterns.

45. Making patterns

A pattern is a small image, that is being *repeated* inside an area, until that area is filled up with the pattern.

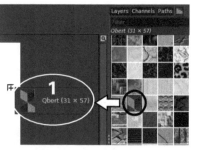

Open the *Patterns* panel by going to the *Configure Tab > Add Tab > Patterns*. To fill a *layer* with a pattern, simply drag a pattern *icon* on the canvas (1, 2).

I will increase the preview size of the pattern thumbnails, by going to the *Configure Tab > Preview size > Enormous*. Now we can see, patterns can have different sizes. They *don't* have to be *square*, and they can have *transparency*. The patterns at the bottom are Gimps default patterns. The patterns above it, are patterns I have downloaded. At the end of this lesson, I will show you where you can download free patterns.

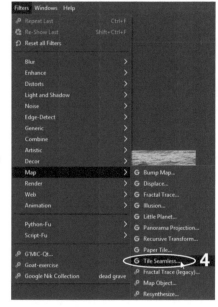

You can also make a pattern yourself. Let's make a water pattern. Open 'Water'. Crop out a piece of water that looks interesting (3). Next we have to make the pattern *seamless*. This means that the pattern can be repeated, in a way that there will be no transitions visible between the tiles.

I will use a *filter* for this. I go to: *Filters > Map > Tile Seamless* (4).

Now the pattern is seamless (5).

To place the pattern in the *Patterns* panel, we have to save it. I go to: *File > Export As*. I will name it `water`. At the bottom, I click on *Select File Type* (5), and scroll down until I see: *GIMP pattern* (6). I select it. At the top I see my file now ends with: *.pat*. I save the pattern

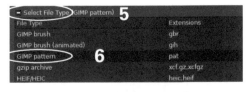

in the *patterns* folder that is inside the *2.10* folder. At the bottom I click on *Export*. Then I click on *Export* again (7). Now I click on the *Refresh patterns* button (8) in the *Patterns*

panel, and the water pattern is added to the panel. I drag it on the canvas to see the result (9). You can *delete* a pattern, by clicking on the little cross (10).

I have downloaded several patterns from *textures.com*. You have to subscribe to download textures. I have a free subscription, which gives a limitation in the amount of textures I can download per day. Let's say I'm looking for a *grass* pattern. At the top there is a search field. I type `grass` (11).

When you hold your mouse above a texture, you can see whether the texture is *seamless*, which means you can directly use it as a pattern (12). When you click on a texture, you can download it. The downloaded file will be a *.jpg* file. Because *.jpg*, *.png*, *.gif*, and *.tiff* files can also be used as a pattern, you can place the jpg file *directly* in the *patterns* folder that is inside the *2.10* folder.

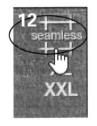

In the next lesson we will look at making duotone images.

46. Making duotone images

A duotone image is an image that is built up of two colors, normally a single color, and black. Duotone is often used to create a *sepia effect*, which is a brownish tinted black and white, for an old look.

I have opened 'Amsterdam'. I'll first lighten up the image with *Levels*.

Now I would like to give this image an old look, a sepia effect. I go to: *Colors > Colorize*. I drag the *Hue* to a brownish color (1). I will *desaturate* the color a bit by dragging *Saturation* to the left (2).

Now let's use duotone to get a modern look. I have opened *Office_buildings.jpg*. I go to: *Colors > Colorize*. I will choose a blue color. You can click on *Preview* to compare (3).

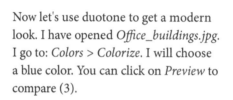

In the last example I will colorize a face by combining *Colorize* and *Curves*. Open 'Girl_Close-up'. I will use green this time. I will first give it maximum *Saturation* (4). I will lower the *Lightness* (5), so I'm not losing too much detail in the *highlights*. I click on *OK*. Now I open *Curves*. I will increase the *contrast* by giving the curve a *'S'* form (6). Now I have a cartoony like duotone (7).

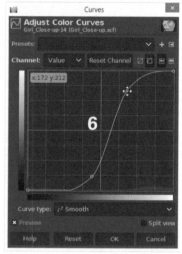

Now open 'Girl_duotone'. Another way to get interesting duotone images, is by using the *Hard mix* blending mode. *Hard Mix* will change colors to either: *red, green, blue, white, or black.* Above the girl layer, I make a new empty layer, and set it on *Hard mix*. I Select the *Gradient* tool. In the *Tool Options*, I will select the preset *Yellow Orange*. I drag over the canvas.

Dragging the endpoints will give different results. You can *edit* the colors, *add* colors, and *edit* them again.

In the next lesson we will look at how to save in the PDF format.

47. Saving as a PDF

The PDF format is a globally used format for sharing digital content, that contains both *images* and *text*. PDF stands for *Portable Document Format*. Text in a PDF document can be *real* text (so not pixels). This means text can often be *copied* from a PDF document. The PDF format is not only optimized for viewing on the *screen*, but *also* for *print*. In the printing industry, the PDF format is preferred for printing. Also, regardless which size you print, the *text* will always be sharp.

In Gimp, you can save in the PDF format. Let's create a document with some text, and open it in Acrobat Reader. Create a new document. Select the text

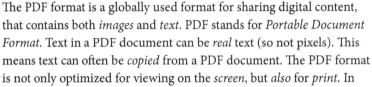

tool, and drag a text frame. Type some text. To save the file as a PDF, go to: *File > Export As*. At the top you can give the file a name. Navigate to the location where you want to save the PDF. At the bottom left click on *Select File Type*. Scroll down to: *Portable Document Format* and click on it (1). Then click on *Export*. You're asked if you want to: *Apply layers masks, Convert images to vectors*, and *Omit hidden layers* (2). I want the *first* and *last* option, and click on *Export* (3). For complex files with layers that use *blending modes*, it is advisable to first *merge all pixel layers* to a *single layer*, and *above* place the *text layers*, before creating the PDF.

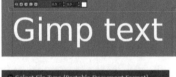

Let's open the PDF in Acrobat Reader. No matter how far we zoom in on the text, the text will *always* stay sharp (4). New in Gimp 2.10 is the ability to save a PDF with *multiple pages* (5). When you select this option, all content that is *inside* a layer Group, will become one *single page*, so *each* layer Group is one page. And each *layer* that is *not* inside a layer Group, will *also* become a separate page.

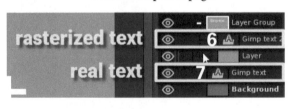

All the *text* that is *inside* a layer group, however, will be *rasterized* (6). So text *inside* a layer Group will become pixels, and text *outside* a layer Group will

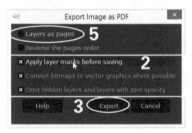

stay *selectable text* in the PDF (7). So if you want *selectable* text, visible *together* with images on a page, you can *only* do this with a *single page* PDF. This means, *Layers as pages* (5) should *not* be checked.

In the next lesson we will look at how to save to the Photoshop format.

48. Saving as a Photoshop file

Gimp can *open* Photoshop native *.psd* files, and *save* Photoshop *.psd* files. Gimp reads layers, masks, and paths. In the Gimp 3.2 release Gimp will also have layer Styles and Adjustment layers (and probably will be able to read them). For this reason, when you open a *.psd* file into Gimp that comes from Photoshop, Adjustment layers and layer Styles are ignored, which can be solved by turning layer Styles into *separate layers*, and to *apply* Adjustment layers in Photoshop, before saving a *.psd* file.

To turn a layer Style, for example a drop shadow, into a separate layer, in Photoshop you *right-click* on the layer Style and choose: *Create Layer* (1). Now the drop shadow is on its own layer (2).

And before you *apply* an Adjustment layer (for example a Levels adjustment) to a layer, *make a copy* of that layer first so you stay flexible and have an original. You can hide the original layer (3).

In Gimp, to *save* in the *.psd* format, go to: *File > Export As*. At the bottom left click on: *Select File Type*. Scroll down to *Photoshop image*, and select it (4). Now your file name will show *.psd* at the end. Click on *Export* at the bottom right to save the file. The file can be opened in Photoshop with layers, masks, and paths intact.

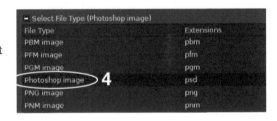

In the next chapter we will explore the *Google Nik Collection* plugin suite.

Chapter 5

Google plugins

49. Download and installing

The *Nik Collection* is a *high-end* photo editing plugin suite, used by professional photographers all over the world.

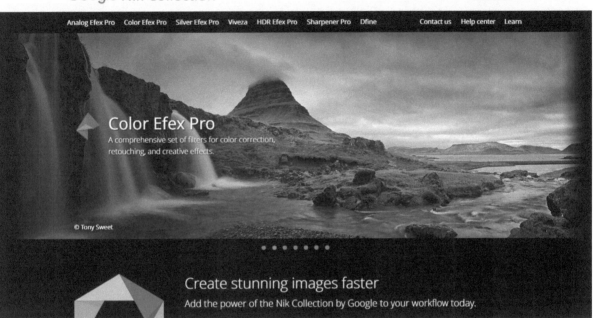

This photo enhancement software comes from a software development company called *Nik Software*, which was established in 1995. The *Nik Collection* suite was originally sold for $500. In 2012 Google acquired Nik Software, to integrate the company into the Google Plus social media platform.

In 2016 Google announced that they will make the entire Google Nik Collection a *free* download, in order to get unique and powerful photo editing tools, once only used by professionals, out to more people.

The Nik Collection can be downloaded from *www.google.com/nikcollection*. Click on the blue download button (1). The Google Nik Collection can also be downloaded here from Udemy, it is attached to this lecture. After downloading, in your *Downloads* folder, you can *double-click* on the file to install it (2).

In the next lesson we will start making global adjustments with Nik's *Viveza 2*.

50. Making global adjustments

The heart of the Nik Collection, is its patented single-click selection method, called *U-Point technology*. Using the U-Point technology, you can select an object, simply by *clicking* on it. The selection you get, gives photo-realistic results. The U-Point technology makes photographic editing fast, easy, and intuitive, as we will see in the *next* lesson.

In this lecture we will explore the interface of the Nik software, and start with making *global* adjustments. In the next lecture, we will look at *local* adjustments using the *U-Point* technology.

Open *Beach.jpg*. As we can see the image is overexposed. I will open the image in Nik's *Viveza 2*, in which we can adjust Value, color, and structure with easy-to-use sliders.

To open the image in *Viveza 2*, go to: *Filters > Google Nik Collection* (1). In the window that opens, behind *Program*, you can choose a Nik plugin. *DFine 2*, which is a powerful *noise removal* plugin, is shown by default. Click on it, and from the drop-down list, choose *Viveza 2* (2).
Behind *Layer* I will leave *new from visible* selected (3). This way I won't overwrite my image, and will receive a *new layer* with the Nik adjustments on it. I click on OK.

When Viveza opens, you can press *F* to work in *full screen mode*. Right now we see four sliders: *Brightness*, *Contrast*, *Saturation*, and *Structure* (4). *Structure* is developed and patented by Nik Software, and we will look at it in a moment.
If you click on the *Expand all sliders* icon (5), you get six more sliders. You can use *all* sliders. To quickly set a slider back to 0%, just *double*-click on the slider triangle.
Warmth works the same way as *temperature* found in programs like *Lightroom*. Dragging it to the left, makes the image look colder, dragging it to the right, makes the image look warmer.

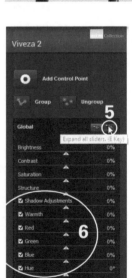

Shadow Adjustments is a powerful way to brighten up the *darkest* areas of an image, like the deep shadows below (7, 8).

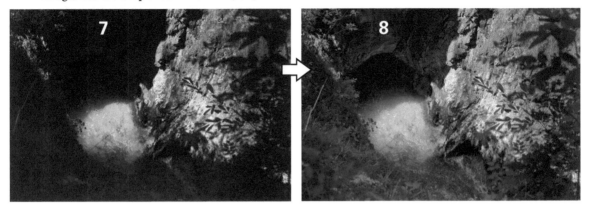

With *Structure* you are able to control the amount of *detail* that is visible in an image. Let's see what *Structure* can do for our *overexposed background*. I drag *Structure* to the right (9, 10).

To toggle between a *100%* view, and seeing the *entire* image, just *double-*click on the image. When you press the *spacebar*, you see a *hand* appearing. With the spacebar pressed down, you can pan through the image by *dragging*.

At the top you can click on *Preview*. On the bottom right, click on *Save*. In Gimp, we now get a *new* layer, with the *adjusted* image. Let's compare the sand. We can see the difference that *Structure* has brought (11, 12).

In the next lesson we will start making *local* adjustments using the *U-Point* technology.

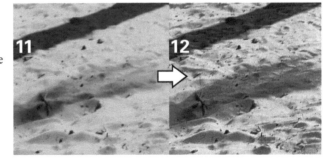

51. Making local adjustments

In this lecture we will look at making local adjustments using the *U-Point technology*. Open *Beach_local.jpg*. In this image I want to bring some texture back in the white sand. I go to: *Filters > Google Nik Collection*. I will use *Viveza 2* again.

I want to adjust *only* the sand. To select the sand, I click on the *Add Control Point* button (1). Now I click in the sand. The small circle at the top left, is the *Control point* (2). You

can drag the *Control point* around. Below the *Control point* are the same *10 sliders* we also find at the right. And with the *top* slider (at the right of the *Control point*) you can *increase* or *decrease* the *area of influence*, which is the thin circle (3, 4).

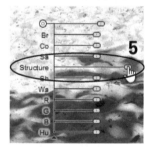

Inside this circle, the *sand* is selected. I will increase the *area of influence* by dragging the slider to the right, so that *all* the sand is selected (4). Now I will increase the *Structure* (5). When you click on *Preview* at the top, you can see *only* the sand has been adjusted in the image (selected with just a single click!) (6).

Let's place another *Control point*. I click on the *Add Control Point* button again, and click in the sky (7). I can now lighten the sky, inside the area of influence.

I drag the *Brightness* slider (8). To select more of the sky, I make the *area of influence* larger (9). I can click on the *sand Control point* to work on the sand, and click on the *sky Control point* to work on the sky. If I click on: *Control Point List* at the right (10), I can see my two Control points; *Control Point1*, and *Control Point2*.

I am also able to see the *mask* that *Viveza* has made, by clicking on: *Show / hide selection of Control Point*, at the right of Control point 1 (11).
This is the selection for the *sand* (12).

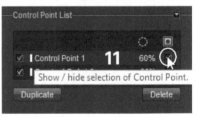

I deselect the *Show / hide selection of Control Point* for Control point 1, and select it for Control point 2 (13).
We can now see the selection for the *sky* (14).

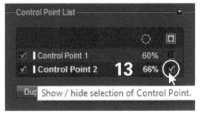

I will click on *Save*. In Gimp we now have the *original*, and *adjusted* layer. This means we are still able to bring some areas *back* to the original image by using a layer *mask*. I *right*-click on the adjusted layer on top, and choose: *Add Layer Mask*. I fill it with white. If I want to *remove* an adjusted area, I can paint with

black on the mask. If I lower the *Opacity* of the brush, I remove only partially, and start *blending* the layers.

Let's explore *Control points* a bit further. Open *Girl_crop.jpg*. I would like to make the face and the arms of the girl a bit lighter. I go to: *Filters > Google Nik Collection*. This time, I will open the image in *Color Efex Pro 4* (15). Color Efex is a *filter collection* with more than 50 filters. It is used for color corrections, retouching and creative effects.

When you open *Color Efex*, the last filter you used, which in my case is the *Sunlight filter*, is shown at the right (16). We'll look at the *Sunlight filter* in the next lesson.

At the left side you can choose a filter (17). Each filter has several presets, from which you can choose. Click on the *preset mode icon* at the right of a filter (18) to see the presets for that filter.

Click on a preset to use it (19).
To exit the preset mode, click on the *Back* button (20) to go to *list mode* and see all filters displayed again.

Right now we see *all* 55 filters (21). If I click on, for example, the *Landscape* tab, I see the filters that are closely related to Landscape images. I like to see all the filters, so I click on *ALL*.

At the right, I will *remove* the *Sunlight* filter, by clicking on the little *cross* at the right (22). Now I see my image without any adjustments.

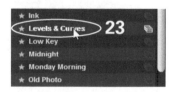

The filter I will use for the image, is *Levels & Curves*. I click on it (23).

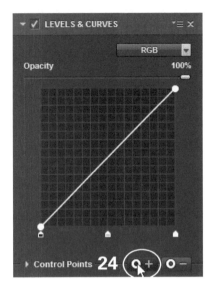

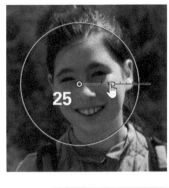

In *Color Efex*, the *Control Points* are placed at the bottom of a filter. There are two types of Control Points in Color Efex; *plus* Control Points and *minus* Control Points. The *plus* Control point is a *normal* control point. We will look at the *minus* Control Point in a moment. I click on the *Control Point button* that has a *plus* sign, to add a Control Point (24). I place a Control Point on the girls face, and adjust the area of influence (25).

If I now adjust the Curve at the right (26), I will see I am only adjusting the Value of the girls face. Now let's also brighten up her right arm. I can place a new Control Point, but I can also *reuse* the Control Point I already have, by *duplicating* it.

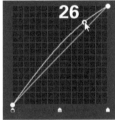

You can *duplicate* a control point in *three* ways:

1) by pressing *Ctrl-D*

(I can *delete* the duplicate again by pressing *Delete* or *Backspace*).

2) Click on the text: *Control Points*. You now have a *Duplicate* and *Delete* button (27). First select the Control Point you want to duplicate. Then click on the *Duplicate* button (at the left of the trash can).

I will delete the duplicate again.

3) The third way is the *fastest* way. When you hold down *Alt*, and then *drag* a Control Point, you duplicate the Control Point *while you drag!*

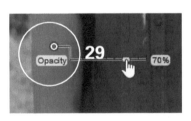

I *Alt*-drag the Control Point from the face to the arm, and adjust the area of influence (28). For the arm, I want to *reduce* the *strength* of the effect a bit. In Color Efex a Control Point has an *Opacity* slider (29). I will drag the *Opacity* down to about 70%.

If you experience undesired *spilling* of a *Control Point* to the surroundings, you can do the following. I will drag the Control Point up to the *top* of the arm, and make the area of influence *smaller*, so the Control Point will only cover the top half of the arm. Now I *Alt*-drag this Control Point to the *lower* part of the arm (30). Again I have the whole arm covered, but now I am using *two smaller* Control Points to do this, which leads to less spilling.

To adjust the light on this *arm*, it would be efficient to have *both* Control Points to *act as one*. I can do this by *grouping* the Control Points. To *group* Control Points, I start by selecting the Control Points that I want to group. You select Control Points by *Shift*-clicking on them. The *first selected*

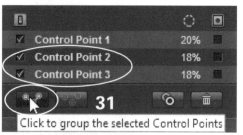

Control Point becomes the Control Point that will control the *other* Control Points of the group. When you have all Control Points selected, click on the *Click to group the selected Control Points* button (31).

I now have a *group* of Control Points, named: *Group1* (32).

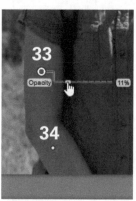

If I now adjust the *main* (the first selected) Control Point (33), I am also changing the *other* Control Point (34).
If you want to *ungroup* a group again, select the group (35), and click on the *Click to ungroup Control Points* button (36).

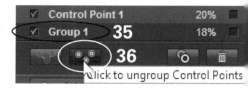

I will also *Alt*-drag a Control Point over to the girl's *left* arm.

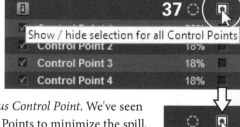

Now let's have a look at the *minus Control Point*. We've seen how to *combine smaller* Control Points to minimize the spill, if needed. If this wouldn't be enough, you can also use *minus* Control Points. To show how they work, we will look at the *masks* themselves. At the right I click on *Show / hide selection for all Control Points* (37). We now can see the masks (38).

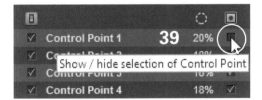

You can *show* and *hide* *individual* Control Points, by clicking on the *Show / hide selection of Control Point* icons. Let's hide the Control Point for the *face* (39, 40). I will reveal the selection of the face again, by clicking on the icon again.

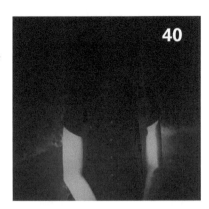

To remove the light spill we have, I will now place a *minus* Control Point. I click on the *Add a Control Point set to 0%*

Opacity button (41), and then I click at the *left* of the girls face. I will increase the area of influence (42).

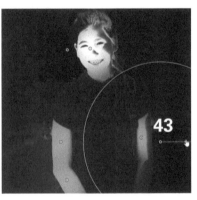

I can do the same at the bottom. I click on the *minus* Control Point button again, and click at the right of her arm (43). And lastly, I place a minus Control Point at the left side of her arm, to subtract from the selection (44). I click twice on the *Show / hide selection for all Control Points* icon, to exit mask view again.

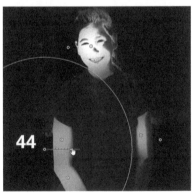

Now I have a very refined mask. If I adjust the curve (45), I see *only* the face and arms are affected (46).
Now let's say I want to make the skin tone a bit *warmer*. I could

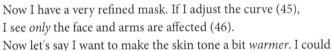

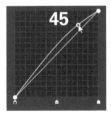

The Ultimate Gimp 2.10 Guide **165**

go into the *Red*, *Green* and *Blue* color channels of the filter and adjust them (47), but I will use *another filter* for this; the *Brilliance / Warmth* filter. You can add a new filter in *two* ways. The first method is to click (below the filters at the right) on the *Add Filter* button (48).

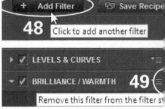

Then go to the left side and choose a filter by clicking on it. I'll *delete* the placed filter again by clicking on the little cross (49). With the second method you can *skip* the *Add Filter* button, and directly add a new filter by *Shift*-clicking on it.

When you use this second method to add a filter, be careful not to click on a filter *without* holding Shift, because this will *remove* the last added filter. When this happens you can press *Ctrl-Z* to undo.

I will use the fast method, and *Shift*-click on *Brilliance / Warmth* (50). The filter is now added to the filter list.

There is also a *History panel* (51). Click on the tab to open it. I will drag the slider to the bottom. We can see the *last*

action is: *Brilliance / Warmth added* (52). Like in Gimp, you can *select* an earlier state, and continue from there. To exit the *History Panel*, click at the top on the Color Efex Pro 4 tab.

What I would like to do is to *reuse* the Control Points that I made with Levels and Curves.
To do this, I go to Levels and Curves.
To select *all* Control Points, I can *drag* over the entire image, or I can press *Ctrl-A* (which is faster). To *copy* the selected Control Points, I click on the menu icon at the right (53), and choose: *Copy Control Points*. Now I go to *Brilliance / Warmth*. I click on the menu icon at the right of Brilliance / Warmth, and choose: *Paste Control Points* (54). I have now *copied* the Control Points over.

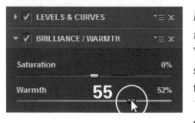

When I drag the Warmth slider to the right (55), I am *only* making the *skin* warmer. I can *show* and *hide* the Brilliance / Warmth filter by clicking on the *check mark* at the left of the filter name (56).

To *zoom in* press the space bar. To *zoom out*, press the space bar again. You can change the *zoom percentage* at the top by clicking on the triangle icon (57). To *pan*, like in *Viveza 2*, hold the spacebar pressed down, and drag with your mouse.

52. Using recipes

If I want to continue working on the image at a later point, I can save my work as a *Recipe*. The *Save Recipe* button is at the bottom right (1). I can save in two ways: *with*, or *without* the Control Points included. To save *with* the Control Points, press *Shift* when you click on the *Save Recipe* button. I will *Shift*-click on the button.

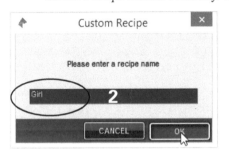

I type a name for the *Recipe* (2), and click on OK.

The *Recipes menu* opens at the left. My *Recipe* (called `Girl`) is displayed (3).

Now I can continue working on the image at a later point. My settings are saved. At the bottom right I click on *Save* (4), to open the image in Gimp.

An image saved from *Color Efex* will give a *TIFF image Message* (5). The message tells that the image has been transferred from *Color Efex* to *Gimp* in the high quality *TIFF* format (which is what we want). You can just press the *space bar* and the message disappears.

Now let's say I want to *continue* working in *Color Efex* with my image. Because the *top visible* layer will be opened when you use a Google filter, you can either drag the *original* layer to the top (6), or hide the layer(s) above it.

I go to *Filters > Google Nik Collection*. The last filter that I used *(Color Efex)* is still selected, so I click on OK. I go to the *Recipes*, I click on the saved *Recipe* called `Girl`. I'm warned that the *Recipe* will *replace* any *current* filters at the right (7). I click on Yes. Now I can continue working on the image, with my *saved settings*.

Click to update this recipe

When I'm finished and leave Color Efex, and I want to *save* my settings *again*, I can:

1) create a *new* Recipe, or
2) I can *update* the *existing* Recipe.

To *update* a Recipe, click on the *update button* at the bottom right of the Recipe Thumbnail (8).

I can also *delete* a Recipe, by clicking at the *top left* (9). And I can *save* a Recipe on my hard drive, for *back-up* and for *sharing*, by clicking on the *top right* (10).

In the next lesson we will explore some more *filters* in *Color Efex Pro 4*.

53. Adjusting color and structure

Color Efex Pro has 55 filters. Google has a Nik Collection *YouTube* channel, where each filter of Color Efex is discussed separately. You can find the YouTube channel at: *www.youtube.com/user/NikSoftwareLessons*
You can also visit Googles website: *the Nik Collection by Google Help Center* at: *https://support.google.com/nikcollection*.

In this lesson I will discuss some filters to get you started. I start with three filters that make images look warmer.

In the last lecture we've already used the *Brilliance / Warmth* filter to warm up the skin of the girl. A filter related to it, is the *Sunlight Filter*. Open *Sun_forest.jpg*. I would like to add some sunlight to this image. I select the *Sunlight* filter (1). I can adjust the *Light Strength*, the *Light Temperature*, as well as the *Brightness*, *Contrast*, and *Saturation*. We now have a sunnier image (2).

The next warming filter is the *Skylight Filter* (3). Open *Woman_beach.jpg*. The *Skylight Filter* removes blue casts and warms the image up (4).

With the *Foliage Filter* (5), you can bring the *greens* in nature images, to life. There are three presets. I will choose *Method 2*. With *Enhance Foliage* you can set the strength of the filter.

Now we will look at two interesting *color correction* filters. Open *Bride.jpg*. To color correct this image, and remove the *blue color cast* from the wedding dress, I will select the *White neutralizer filter*. At the right, I select the color picker (6). When I click on the dress (7), the blue color cast will be removed (8). At the left of the color picker, I can see the color I have chosen to become *neutral*. The *White neutralizer filter* is more flexible than the *Pick grey point* picker from *Levels* in Gimp.

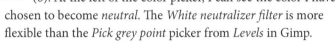

Another interesting color correction filter is *Remove Color Cast* (9). Open *Town.jpg*. By dragging the Color slider, you can quickly find the best point for *neutralising* the color cast.

In the previous lesson we've seen *Structure* in action in *Viveza*. *Color Efex* goes further, and offers *six contrast* filters, which are all based on the *Structure* algorithm. Let's have a look.

If you want a more dramatic look in an image, you can use *Dark contrasts* (10). Open *mountains_snow.jpg*. I will increase *Contrast*, *Dark Detail*, and *Brightness*. With *Shadows / Highlights protection*, you can reduce the effect in the Shadows and/or Highlights if needed.

The next filter is *Contrast Only*. Open *Rose.jpg*. With *Contrast Only* you have control over *how* contrast is applied. You have *Normal Contrast* (11) followed by *Contrast Only* (12), which prevents *colors* from being *affected*, and *Soft Contrast* (13),

which gives *softer transitions*. When I select the *Dark Contrasts* (14) filter, we see we get a totally different result. *Contrast Only* is often used for food photography.

Another contrast filter is *Contrast color range* (15). I have opened *Bride_and_groom.jpg*. The color selected with *Color*, will cause objects

of that color to become *lighter*, while opposite, or *complementary* colors will become *darker*.

This is a quick and effective way, to get better contrast between the bride and groom, and the background.

With *Dark contrasts*, we made *lighter* areas *darker*, to give them more drama. With *Pro Contrast*, we do the opposite, and dynamically *lighten up* areas in a *dark image*.
I have opened *Flowers.jpg*. We can see the flowers much better now (16).

With *Detail extractor*, you can bring out detail in an image in *three* ways.
Open *Ocean_rocks.jpg*. Under *Effect Radius*, you can adjust the *fine* detail (17), the *medium* detail (18), or the *Larger* detail (19) *separately*.
And finally, with *Tonal contrast*, you can bring out detail in the *Highlights*,

Midtones, or *Shadows* separately. There are also *five* Contrast Types you can choose from: *Standard* (20), *High Pass* (21), *Fine* (22), *Balanced* (23), and *Strong* (24).

In this lesson, we have used the filters globally. For more *refined* results, you can use the *Control Points*.

In the next lesson we will look at *creative* filters.

54. Using creative filters

To get a different look and feel for your image, *Color Efex* has several creative filters, like the *Bleach bypass* filter. Open *Pub.jpg*. The Bleach bypass filter simulates a technique from the days of color film, where the bleaching step was skipped. This results in a high contrast, low saturation look (1).

For more creative filters, we will now go to *Analog Efex Pro 2*, which is the plugin for special effects. This plugin can be very useful for giving a *book cover* a special look. Open *The man on the train.xcf*. I *right*-click on the top layer and choose: *New from Visible*, (2) to get a single layer I can open in *Analog Efex*. Then I go to: *Filters > Google Nik Collection*. I choose *Analog Efex Pro 2*, and click on OK.

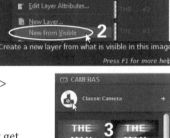

At the left, there are some presets (3). From the presets we can already get some interesting ideas for an effect, which can then be fully modified at the right side. *Analog Efex*, like *Color Efex*, works with *stackable* effects.

To get to the *individual* filters, click on the *Classic Camera* icon (4).

Below *Tools*, we see the filters of *Analog Efex*. Let's have a look at *Light Leaks* (5). I click on it.

With *Light Leaks* (6) you can add a *light flare* to your image.

There are many Light Leaks to choose from. There are: *Soft*, *Crisp*, and *Dynamic* leaks (7).

You can *position* a light leak, by dragging the blue circle (8).

At the top, you can set the *Strength* of the Light Leak (9).

As in Color Efex, you will *replace* an effect if you click on another affect at the left. To *add* an effect in Analog Efex, you click on the *plus* icon, at the right of an effect (10). I will add: *Zoom & Rotate Blur*.

To remove an effect, click on the *minus* icon (11).

With *Zoom & Rotate Blur*, I can bring some movement to text and images. The inner circle is the *effect free area* (12), and between the inner and outer circle is the *transition* area (13).

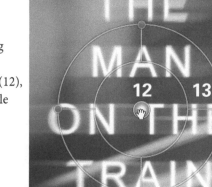

I can adjust the *size* of the *inner*, and the *outer* circle (14, 15). I can also *rotate* the *outer* circle (16).

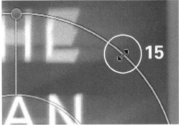

I can reposition the whole effect with the blue middle point (17).

I can also use the *sliders* at the right (18).

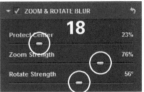

Because I want to distort *only* the *text*, and *not* the background, I'll press Cancel. In Gimp, I delete the top layer (that Analog Efex returned). I want to make a layer with *only* text visible, on a *black* background. To do this, I place *above* the layer(s) that I don't want to be distorted an new layer, and fill it with black. Above this black layer I place the *text* layers that I want to adjust. Then I *right*-click on the top layer, and choose: *New from Visible*. Now I have a *single* layer with *only* text, on a *black* background (19). The black background will *disappear* later again, when I set the result (coming from Analog Efex) on the *Screen* blending mode. Doing this, I am able to place the

adjusted text in front of the unaffected image(s).

I go to: *Filters > Google Nik Collection*, and click on OK. I click on the *Classic Camera* icon, and select the *Zoom & Rotate Blur* filter. I will add some motion to the text. Then I click on Save.

In Gimp I will now *hide* the *original* text layers (for backup). I will also delete the *black* layer, and the *New from Visible* layer. I set the layer that *Analog Efex* returned, on the *Screen* blending mode. Now we see the result (20).

Next, let's add some motion to an *image*. For a thriller book-cover, I open *Barn.jpg*. I go to: *Filters > Google Nik Collection*, and open *Analog Efex*. I click on the *Classic Camera* icon, and select the *Zoom & Rotate Blur* filter again.

I drag the midpoint on the tree (21) and rotate the blur a bit. I click on Save.

A related blur effect is *Motion blur*. Open *Race_car.jpg*. I would like to bring some motion blur into this image. I go to: *Filters > Google Nik Collection*, and open *Analog Efex*. I click on the *Classic Camera* icon, and select the *Motion Blur* filter. As with *Zoom & Rotate Blur*, you have the *effect free* area (22), and the *transition* area (23). With the small circle (24) you set *both* the direction (or *Angle*), *and* the *Strength* of the motion blur (longer distance means stronger blur). Independent of this *main* blur control, you can also add *seven additional* Blur Points, to tweak the result. With these additional Blur Points, you can control the Angle and Strength in a certain *area* (25). To delete an additional Blur Point, select it and press *Delete*.

I have already *saved* a finished motion blur effect for this race car (26). The *preset*, which is called a *Recipe* in Color Efex, can be found in the *Custom* panel. I named my Recipe: Race-car. I click on it (26).

I have placed the main control at the top (27), and used all seven additional Blur Points, to tweak the result locally.

To have the *driver free* of blur, I placed a blur point *on* the driver, and dragged the dot at the end of the arrow *fully in*.

To *save* a *preset* in *Analog Efex*, click on the *Save* preset button (28). Like in *Color Efex*, to save a preset with Control Points included, you *Shift*-click. And you can also *update*, *delete*, and *export* the preset.

Finally, we will look at *Bokeh*. Open *Town_at_night.jpg*. Go to: *Filters > Google Nik Collection*, and open *Analog Efex*.

Again, there is an *effect free* area, and a *transition* area (29).

 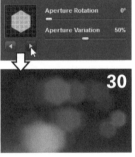

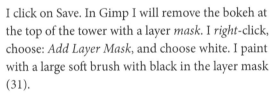

You can change the look of the bokeh (30).

I click on Save. In Gimp I will remove the bokeh at the top of the tower with a layer *mask*. I *right*-click, choose: *Add Layer Mask*, and choose white. I paint with a large soft brush with black in the layer mask (31).

I have now added some depth to my image using the *Bokeh* filter (32).

In the next lesson we will look at making Vignettes.

55. Making vignettes

A vignette normally is a darkening of the edges of an image. It can be added to draw the attention of the viewers eye to the subject in the middle. In this lesson we will look at some vignette filters and image borders in *Color Efex*. Open *Bird_1.jpg*. Go to: *Filters > Google Nik Collection*, and open *Color Efex*.

At the left, select *Vignette Filter*. *Transition* (1) is the distance between the *inner* and *outer* circle, as we saw in *Analog Efex*.

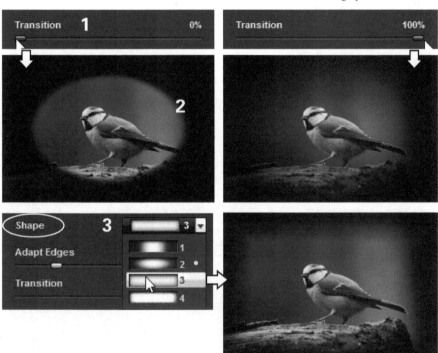

If I drag the *Transition* slider to the left, I get a smaller transition area (2). With *Size* I adjust the size of the effect *free* area (the *inner* circle). With *Opacity* I adjust the strength, or *opacity* of the vignette. With *Shape* (3), you can choose different shapes for the vignette.

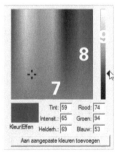

You can adjust the *color* of the vignette.
With the *color picker* (4) you can pick a color from your image (5). If you click on the color *thumbnail* (6), you can manually *adjust* the color. From left to right is *Hue* (7), from top to bottom is *Saturation* (8). And at the right is the *Value* slider, with which you can make a color lighter or darker (9).

Adapt Edges looks at the image and tries to *refine the shape* for the vignette.

For the second vignette filter, *Vignette Lens*, open *Bird_2.jpg*. *Vignette Lens* simulates natural vignettes created by different types of *lenses*. I can transition the Shape from more Circular (10) to

more Rectangular (11). I can adjust the *Size* of the vignette. With *Amount* I can make the vignette darker, or *lighter*. As a result, I can *invert* the vignette, creating a *light vignette* (12).

I can *reposition* the *center* of the vignette. I click on the *Place Center* icon (13), and click in the middle of the bird (14).

I can also place a *minus control point* to *remove* an area of the vignette. I click on the *minus control point* icon, and click on the *eye* of the bird (15).

Another vignette filter is *Vignette blur*. Open *Portrait.jpg*. With *Vignette blur*, you *defocus* the detail around the center of the image, drawing the eye to the subject.

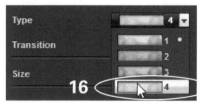

There are four different blur types you can choose from. *Type 4* blurs to white (16, 17).

I will make the transition a bit *less soft* (18), and increase the size a bit.

I click on the *Place Center icon*, and click on her face, to put the girl in the center of the vignette (19). In Gimp, I could *crop* the image again.

The *Darken / Lighten center* vignette filter is a much more *subtle* way of vignetting. It gives *depth* to an image in a *natural* way.
With *Border Luminosity* you can darken or lighten the edges of the image (20). And with *Center Luminosity* you determine the brightness of the center of the image.
With *Center Size* you make the border smaller or larger.

Color Efex also has some adjustable *image borders*. I click on the *Recipes* tab. At the bottom I select *Vintage Saturation* (21). I get a warning that adding this Recipe will replace the filters at the right (22). I click on Yes.

This Recipe has four filters working together. On top the image is given more *contrast*. Below is *Vignette Lens*, to give the image a vignette. Then we have an *image border*. And at the bottom we can see that also *Film Grain* has been added.

Let's take a look at *Film Grain*.

I will zoom in to 200%. I can increase the size of the *grain* if I want to, by dragging *Grain per pixel* to the left (23).

The grain makes the image look like it was shot with *film* (24).

Above *Film Grain* are the *Image borders*. There are 14 image borders to choose from.

You can make an image border more rough or less rough (25). With *Spread* you can *thicken* the edge (26).
And with *Size*, you can move the edge inwards or outwards (27).

In the next lesson we will look at how to make black and white images in *Silver Efex Pro*.

56. Making black and white images

Silver Efex Pro is often considered to be the most powerful black and white plugin on the market, and is used by many professional photographers. With *Silver Efex Pro*, you can make professional looking black and white images, in just a few clicks. Open *Castle.jpg*. Open *Silver Efex Pro*. By default you get a *neutral* black and white conversion (1). By dragging the *Structure* slider, the detail of the image comes out (2).

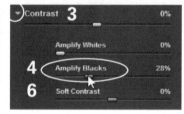

If I click on the triangle in front of *Contrast* (3), I get *more options* for adjusting Contrast. I can now amplify the *whites* and *blacks* separately.

I will amplify the *blacks* a bit (4, 5). I will also add some *Soft Contrast* (6), to bring more *depth* to the image (7).

To compare, I can not only click on the *Compare* button, but I can also select *Split preview* (8). I can now drag a *red line* to the left and the right (9), which lets me quickly compare the before and after. At the right of Split preview is *Side-by-side* preview (10).

In between the images, you can click on the *double arrow* to alternate between seeing the images on top of each other (11),

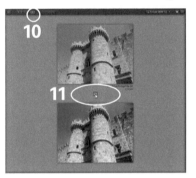

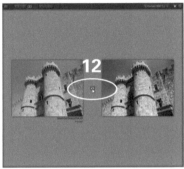

or side by side (12). Split preview and Side-by-side preview are also available in the other Nik plugins.

To create more room for the image, you can *hide* (and show) the tab columns at both sides individually, by clicking on the *Show / Hide icons* (at the left and right side).

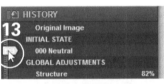

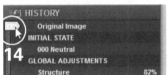

I can also compare to the (original) *color* image. To do this, I click on the *History* tab, and drag the orange slider (13) to the top, to: *Original Image* (14).

To be able to drag the *orange slider* in the History panel, you need to be in *Split preview* or *Side-by-side preview*.

Now let's do something more challenging. Open *Bride_and_groom.jpg*. Go to: *Filters > Google Nik Collection*, and open *Silver Efex*. As we can see, there is not much contrast between the bride and groom, and the background.

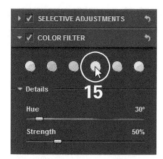

I click on *Color Filter*. Here I can add different color filters. Let's see how they affect the image. Grey is neutral, as we have now. If I use the *Red* (15) or *Yellow* filter, the bride and groom brighten up (16).

Now I click on *Film Types* (17) and open *Sensitivity* (18). Here I can control *per color*, how dark or light that color will be. Dragging to the left makes it darker, to the right brighter. I will increase the *Red* tones, which brightens up the *skin* tones (19). I will also increase *Cyan* and *Blue* to brighten up the *sky* and the *water*. And lastly, I will increase the *Structure* a bit. I click on Save.

In Gimp, I could *also use* this black and white image, to improve the *color* image! I will set it's blending mode to *HSV Value* (20). By adjusting the Opacity, I can determine how *much* I want to *replace* the *Value* from the color layer, with the *improved* Value from the black and white layer (21).

I can even lighten up the *Value* layer a bit with *Levels*. By hiding the top layer, I can see the improvement of the light conditions for the bride and groom.

I will create a single image from the result, by *right*-clicking on the top layer, and choose *New from visible*. I open *Color Efex*. I will use the *Sunlight filter* to give the image a bit more sun, and click on Save. In Gimp can *lower* the Opacity a bit if I want. If I *Shift*-click on the eye of the bottom layer (the layer that I started with) I can now see how the image has improved from the start.

In the next lesson we will look at reducing digital noise with DFine.

57. Remove noise

In this lesson we will look at reducing digital noise. Open *Girl_crop.jpg*. Go to: *Filters > Google Nik Collection*, and open *DFine 2*. When you open the program it will already have already *analysed* and *denoised* the image. It analysed the noise by looking at a couple of low contrast areas. The program shows where it looked, which is *inside* the *white* dotted *squares* (1). Nine out of ten times, this *automatic* noise reduction will give good results, and you can directly click on Save.

However, if you want to, you have more control. You can for example draw your *own* squares (or rectangles) for the program to look at. To do this, behind *Method*, click on *Automatic*, and choose: *Manual* (2). Below, you can now click on the *Add rectangle* button (3), and drag over an important area, that you want to be *denoised* (4).

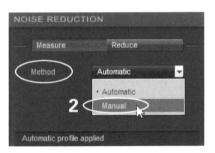

If you click on the *Select* tool (5), you can *move* and *resize* the rectangles. You can also *delete* rectangles by selecting them and pressing the *Delete* key. To delete *all* rectangles click on the *Reset* button.

When you *change* a rectangle, the program will say: *Profile needs to be updated* (6). To make a *new* profile from the *new* rectangles, click on the *Measure Noise* button (7).

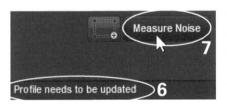

To *zoom* in and out I select the *Zoom* tool (8). My cursor changes to a *magnifying glass* with a *plus* sign (9). If I now click, I zoom in to 300%. To zoom *out* again, I press the *Alt* key, which turns the magnifying glass into a *minus* sign (10). If I now click with the minus sign, I am back to 100%.

If I click one *more* time with the *Alt* key pressed down, I will see the *whole* image. I release the *Alt* key again, and click twice on the girls face to zoom in to 300%.

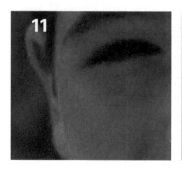
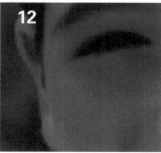

I click on *Preview*, to see the before and after (11, 12). I think the denoising is a little bit too strong on the face, but could be stronger for the background (because the background is *out of focus*, and doesn't have detail).

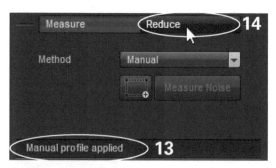

When I read: *Automatic profile applied*, or, *Manual profile applied* (13), I can adjust the denoising by clicking on the *Reduce* button (14).
I can now choose between two methods to adjust the result. I can use *Control points*, or: *Color Ranges*. Let's start with *Color Ranges* (15).

I will click on the top color picker (16), and then click on the cheek of the girl. I have now selected a skin tone (17).

With the *Contrast Noise* slider (18) I now can *decrease* or *increase* the applied noise reduction for *just* the *chosen* color. I will drag the *Contrast Noise* slider to the left (so *under* 100%), to *reduce* the applied noise reduction for the *skin tones*. When I would go *above* 100%, I would *increase* the applied noise reduction for the selected color, even *more*.
Contrast Noise effectively reduces *differences* in *Value* of the selected color.
Color Noise reduction (the slider below) is less noticeable, especially in *jpeg* images, due to the *jpeg compression*.

Now I select the *second* color picker, and click in the green. I will *increase* the noise reduction for the green tones, because they are in the *background*, which is out of focus. You can *add* more color ranges when needed, by clicking on the *plus* icon at the bottom (19).

You can also use *Control points* to adjust the applied noise reduction. The advantage of *Control points* is that you can easily *exclude* areas from being denoised. By using *minus* Control points I can for example exclude the eyes and eyebrows (where the denoising is a bit to strong). I click on the *minus* Control point button (20).

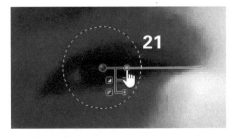

Then I click on the eye, and decrease the area of influence (21).

I *Alt*-drag the *Control point* to the other eye. And I also duplicate it for the eyebrows. The eyes and eyebrows are now *excluded* from the denoising.

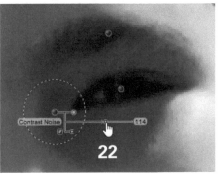

At the right *side* of the nose (in the shadow), I want to *increase* the denoising. To do this I place a normal *(plus)* Control point in the shadow area, and *increase Contrast Noise* by dragging the *Contrast Noise slider* of the Control point to the right (22).

You *deselect* Control points by clicking beside them on the canvas.

After placing the Control points, I am *still* able to increase or decrease the *overall* noise reduction. Let's say I now want to *denoise* the entire image *stronger* (so more than 100%). I do this by dragging the *main Contrast Noise* slider to the right (23). This will not affect the eyes and eyebrows.

In the next lesson we'll look at how to sharpen an image with Sharpener Pro.

58. Sharpening images

In this lecture we will look at how to sharpen an image with *Sharpener Pro 3*. Open *Girl_hair.xcf*. Go to: *Filters > Google Nik Collection*. Under *Program*, we do not only find the *Sharpener* plugin, but also a *pre*-sharpener. The *pre*-sharpener is also called *RAW image sharpener*, and is *only* meant for *RAW* images. RAW is a photo format used by professional photographers. Because RAW images aren't *pre*-sharpened by the camera (like a jpeg is), RAW images first need to be *pre*-sharpened. For more information about pre-sharpening RAW images visit: *www.youtube.com/user/NikSoftwareLessons*.

I open *Sharpener Pro 3*. With *Adaptive Sharpening* (1) you set the *strength* of the sharpening (from 0% to 100%). Below, you determine *how* you sharpen. You can adjust: *Structure*, *Local Contrast*, and *Focus*. I will leave *Adaptive Sharpening* at 100%. Below, with *Output Sharpening Strength*, I can reduce or increase the sharpening strength by dragging the slider below or above 100%. *Higher* than 100% means *increasing* the strength even more.

Right now the image is sharpened. However, I see some noise I don't want. I will *decrease* Structure a bit to reduce the appearance of too much *fine detail*, resulting in smoother surfaces. I will *increase* Local Contrast a bit. Focus *does* make the image sharper, but also introduces the noise again, so I will leave it at 0%. I click on Preview to see the result. The image has become sharper (2).

I can see a light *halo* around the stars in the shadow of the shirt (3). I will place a *Control point*, to *reduce* the halos. I click on the *Add Control Point* button (4), and click on the shadow (*not* on a star!). I adjust the area of influence (5). Now I drag the *Output Sharpening Strength* of the Control point to 0%.

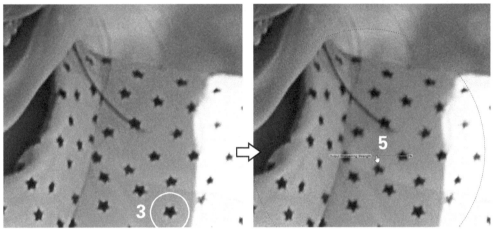

I have now *excluded* the shadow of the shirt from being sharpened. As a result, the halos have disappeared. Because I *only* selected the *shadow* of the shirt, the stars are still sharpened!
When we take a look at the *mask* of the Control point (6), we can see the stars are *not* selected by the Control point. This means they are *not* affected by dragging the *Output Sharpening Strength* of the Control point to 0%.

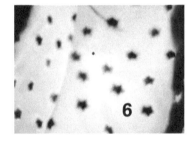

The girl improved by the sharpening, but I liked the background better of the *original*. Back in Gimp, I can quickly restore the background using a layer *mask* (7).

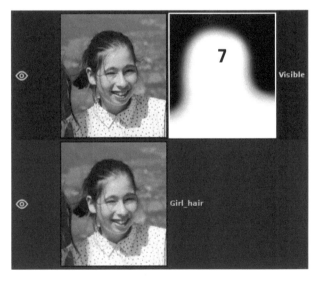

In the next lesson we will look at HDR photography.

59. What is HDR photography?

We've come to the last plugin of the Nik Collection, which is *HDR Efex Pro*. Open *Room_inside.xcf*.

The image of the room has been constructed in *HDR Efex*; it is namely build up from *two* other images. We can see that in this image, *both* the inside of the room, *and* the outside, are well lit.

However, when we look at the original images that I made with my camera, we can see the camera *originally* wasn't able to shoot this.

When I set the camera to have the *inside* well lit, the outside is blown out (1).
And when I focus the camera on having the *outside* well lit, the inside becomes *very* dark (2). Why is this?

The reason for this, is that our *eyes* are about twice as flexible as a camera is. This means, our eyes are able to see a much *wider* range of very dark, up until very light colors (3), than a camera can (4).

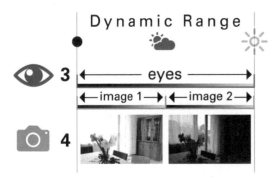

Normally this isn't a problem, and isn't noticeable. But in some situations, for example with a very bright *sun* in the background, combined with deep *shadow* areas, the lower *dynamic range* of the camera can become visible. The deepest blacks, up until the lightest lights, now *can't* be captured by a normal camera *all* at the *same time*. So when you want in a HDR (*High Dynamic Range*) situation, to capture an image that exactly shows what you see with your eyes, you have to make more than one picture. A darker picture, and a lighter picture. Then you *combine* these images in a HDR program.
When you make more than one picture of the same scene, you will need a tripod, to make sure the camera doesn't move between making the different pictures.

If you don't have a tripod, or you have only *one* image from a scene, you can *still* open a single image in *HDR Efex* to improve it. You will get better results though, using different images that together cover the whole light spectrum. When you open a single image, it's best to open a *darker* image, so *without blown out* highlights. Dark areas (because they are still visible) can be recovered to a certain extent. Let's open the *dark* image of the room. I go to: *Filters > Google Nik Collection*, and choose *HDR Efex Pro*. With the default settings, the image improved a lot (5). However the colors suffer to some extent from the image being underexposed, and don't look that natural.

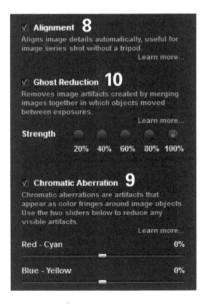

Now let's open *multiple* images of the room. The opening of *multiple* images goes via the plugin itself. I go to: *File > Open images* (6).

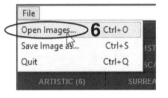

Although you can create an HDR image with just *two* images, HDR programs *prefer* a minimum of *three* images, so with an *extra neutral* image in between the dark, and light image.

I have also added a neutral image. I hold the *Ctrl* key pressed down, and select *Room_dark.jpg*, *Room_medium.jpg*, and *Room_light.jpg* (7). I click on Open.

In the *Merge dialog* window, I will check all three options at the right. The images will now be *Aligned* (8), and color artefacts (*Chromatic Aberration*) are removed (9). When *Ghost Reduction* is checked (10), at the top you can choose *which* image will be the *Ghost Reference Image* (11).

You can choose the *Ghost Reference Image* by dragging the lighter frame over it (12). The *Ghost Reference Image* determines *where* an object will be visible (e.g. a driving car, or a walking person), when that object has *moved* between shooting the images.

✓ Alignment 8
Aligns image details automatically, useful for image series shot without a tripod.
Learn more...

✓ Ghost Reduction 10
Removes image artifacts created by merging images together in which objects moved between exposures.
Learn more...

Strength
20% 40% 60% 80% 100%

✓ Chromatic Aberration 9
Chromatic aberrations are artifacts that appear as color fringes around image objects. Use the two sliders below to reduce any visible artifacts.
Learn more...

Red - Cyan   0%

Blue - Yellow   0%

At the bottom (13), you can adjust the *relative* influence of the images by dragging the scroll bar. I will leave it as it is, so *equally* divided. I click on *Create HDR*.

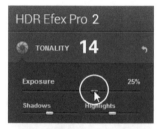

Under *Tonality* (14), I can adjust the *Exposure* to make the image lighter or darker. I will make the image a bit lighter by dragging to the right. I can also adjust the *Shadows* and *Highlights* individually.

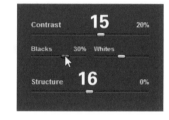

Below, I can adjust the *Contrast* (15), and the *Structure* (16).

With *Tone Compression* (17) I can bring the *Value* (dark and light) tones *closer* to each other. Moving the slider to the right makes *light* tones *darker*, and *dark* tones *lighter*, trying to make all Value tones more *equal*.

Method Strength (18) determines how *strong* the settings, that are below *HDR Method*, are applied. Right now *Depth* (19) is set to *Normal*. I can increase it to *Strong*, or decrease it to *Subtle*.
Detail is by default on *Realistic* (20). To the left makes the detail *softer*, and to the right makes it *stronger*.
Drama (21) is a creative effect. You can give the image a more dramatic look.

Under *Color* (22) you can adjust *Saturation*, color *Temperature*, and *Tint*. *Tint* in conjunction with *Temperature* is often used in programs as Lightroom to *color correct* an image.

Under *Selective Adjustments* you can place *Control Points* to add masks.
Under *Finishing*, you have the *Graduated Neutral Density Filter* (23).
When you have a landscape image where the bright sky is *still* too light,
you can selectively *darken* the top of the image without darkening the rest
of the image. If you drag *Upper tonality* (24) to the left, you darken the top
of the image (25). You can also darken (or lighten) the lower part of the image
with *Lower Tonality*. With *Blend*, you can make the *transition area* larger or
smaller.
With *Vertical Shift*, you can move the whole transition *up*, or *down*.
And with *Rotation*, you can *rotate* the whole filter.
In *Color Efex*, there are several *Graduated Neutral Density Filters* you can use.

To save an image from HDR Efex, whether it is coming from *multiple* images,

or from a *single* image opened via
Gimp, you have to save *via the plugin itself.*
I go to: *File > Save Image As* (26).
I give the file a name (27). I can save
the file as a JPG, or as a TIF. JPG uses
lossy compression, so I will choose TIF
(28). In Gimp, I will open the TIF file,
saved from *HDR Efex*.

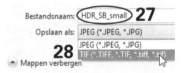

In the next chapter we will look at Retouching.

Chapter 6

Retouching

60. Using the Clone tool

In this chapter we will look at retouching techniques, and the different tools that are available for this.
We start with the *Clone* tool (1). With the *Clone* tool you can copy an area of your image and paste it onto another area. This technique is often used to *remove elements* from an image.

Open 'Organ'. In this image I want to remove the wire at the left of the organ. I click on the *Clone* tool, or press *S* (from *Stamp*). I zoom in to about 300% to have a good view. In the *Tool Options* I will choose a soft brush with 0% hardness. I set the size of the brush to 20 by *Alt-scrolling*. With the *Clone* tool, I will now *copy* pixels from the environment on top of the wire, to make the wire 'disappear'.

To work *non-destructively*, I will work on an *empty* layer *above* the image (2). This way, the cloned pixels (copied from the layer below) are placed on *another* layer, so no pixels are overwritten. The reason I am *able* to clone pixels from *other* layers (than the layer that I am actually working on; the empty layer on top), is because in the *Tool Options*, *Sample merged* has been activated (3). With *Sample merged* checked, everything that is *visible*, is treated as a *single* layer.

What I want, is to *copy* the pixels that are inside the Clone brush (4), and place them *over* the wire.
To do this I first *Ctrl*-click on the place, where I want to copy the pixels from (5). If I now move my mouse to the left (6), I get a *second* circle. The second circle shows me, *where* the pixels from the *first* circle are going to be placed, if I start drawing.

In the first circle (5) you will get to see a little *cross* in the middle of the circle when you hold down the *Ctrl* key. In the second circle (6) you will always see a white *arrow* (that points to the middle of the circle). The cross and the arrow help with *aligning*. Let's say I will use the *horizontal* edge of the beam for *aligning*.
I hold down the *Ctrl* key, and position the *horizontal* line of the cross on the edge of the beam (5). Then I click. Now I release the *Ctrl* key. I move my mouse to the left (6). Inside my second circle, I will point the white arrow to the *same* edge, so that the content of the circles will be perfectly *aligned*.

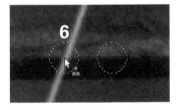

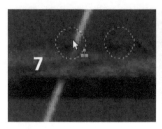 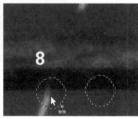

Now I click and drag over the wire (7). I release my mouse. I will also paint over the wire below (8). I have now made a piece of the wire disappear.

Because I have cloned on a *separate* layer, my *original* layer is still intact.

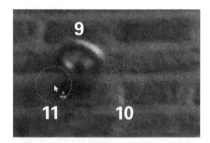

Now let's have a look at the difference between cloning with a *soft* brush, and a *hard* brush.

At the top left, I will remove a pin that's in the wall (9). I zoom in to 300%, and set the brush size to 30. I will first remove the pin with a *soft* brush.

To *align* the clone, I will take the sample at the *top left corner* of a brick (10), and start cloning from the *top left corner* of another brick (11).

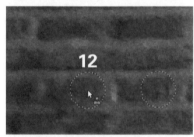

Now I draw over the pin (12). The result with a soft brush looks good.

Now let's do the same with a *hard* brush. By pressing *Ctrl-Z* I undo the cloning.
To get a hard brush, drag *Hardness* to 100% (13).

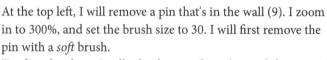

I draw over the pin again. We can see the difference: the hard edge is *visible* (14). Normally, the *larger* the brush, the *softer* the brush needs to be. When you work with a *very small* brush, like size 10, a *hard* brush is the better choice.

In the next lesson, we will let Gimp remove a piece of wire.

61. Remove objects with Heal Selection

We can also let Gimp remove an object for us, using the *Heal selection* filter. Open 'Organ'. Let's remove the wire at the top.

I press *Ctrl-1* to get a 100% view. I tell Gimp which area I want to be removed, by placing a *selection* around it. I click on the *Free Select* tool, and click around the wire to select it (1). I go to: *Filters > Enhance > Heal Selection*.

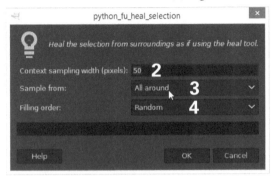

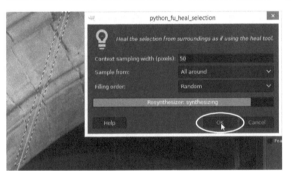

Context sampling width (pixels) (2) determines how far, *around* the selection, the program will look to copy material from. I will leave it at 50 pixels. *Sample from* is by default on *All around* (3). You can also choose to sample from just the *Sides* (so from just the left and right side of the selection), or from *Above and below*. This choice depends on the situation. I will sample from *All around*. *Filling order* is normally best left on *Random* (4). We will explore *Filling order* further in the next example. I click on OK.
I press *Ctrl-D* to deselect.
The wire has been removed (5).

Now open 'Lotus'. In this image (6), I would like to place more focus on the flower. I will do this by creating *depth of field*, by blurring the background. I have already put the flower on a separate layer (7). Let's see what happens when I blur the bottom layer. I go to: *Filters > Blur > Gaussian Blur*. I set the *Blur* radius to about 20, and press *Enter*.
The background is blurred, but I see a white *halo* coming from the flower (8). The reason for this is that the flower *itself* was *also* blurred, and now spreads out. So *before* blurring, I first have to *remove* the flower. To do this, I will use *Heal Selection*.
I press *Ctrl-Z* to undo the blurring.

I *Alt-click* on the top layer to get a selection of the flower. Then I go to: *Filters > Enhance > Heal Selection*. Because *only* the *edge* of the flower becomes visible when we blur, the *edge* is the important part of the filling. For this reason, I now will set *Filling order* to *Inwards towards center* (9). Heal Selection will now *only* look at the *edges*, which gives the best result for the edges (the *center* of the filling however will be ignored). I click on *OK* (10). I press *Ctrl-D* to deselect. I go to: *Filters > Recently Used > Gaussian Blur*, and press *Enter*. The halo is gone (11).

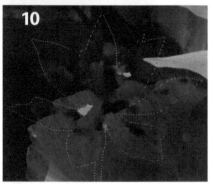

In the last example we will not look at *large* areas, but at *small* ones. Open 'Girl_Close-up'. I will use *Heal Selection* to remove the freckles from the girls nose. I duplicate the layer, and press *B* to select the brush tool. The brush must be *100% hard*. I set the size to 20. I set the Foreground color to *black*, by pressing the *D* key. I press *Q* to go into *Quick mask mode*. I *right*-click at the bottom left on the Quick mask *icon*, and I *invert* the visibility of the mask by choosing: *Mask Selected Areas* (12). As a result of this, the *selected* areas will now show in red. This way I can *see* the face, while I paint the selections in red. All I have to do, is to *click* on the freckles and blemishes that I want to be removed (13). When I'm finished, I press *Q* again to get a *selection* (14). Let's *hide* the selection for a moment. I can *hide* the selection, by going to: *View > Show Selection* (15). The selection is now *still active*, but the 'marching ants' are hidden.

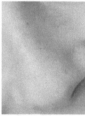

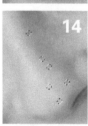

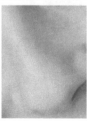

I open *Heal selection* by going to: *Filters > Recently Used > Heal Selection*. Because of the small selections, I think 20 pixels for *Context sampling width* will be enough. So I type: 20, and click on *OK*. Don't forget to turn the *visibility* of the *selection* back on! Go to: *View > Show Selection* again, or press *Ctrl-H* (*H* stands for *Hide*). Now the selection is *visible* again. I press *Ctrl-D* to deselect. By toggling the visibility of the top layer, I can compare the before and after. You could also use this method for restoring *old photos* that have many small damages, or dusts. In the next lesson we will look at a variation of the *Clone* tool, which is the *Heal* tool.

62. Using the Heal tool

The *Clone* an *Heal* tool differ in one essential way: the *Heal* tool doesn't transfer *Hue* and *Saturation*, but only *Value*. Let's have a look.

Open 'Red-green'. The red and green surfaces differ in that the green (1) has variations in darker and lighter green pixels (so *Value* variations), and the red (2) doesn't have this Value variation. Now let's *compare* the Clone and the Heal tool. I start with the *Clone* tool by pressing *S*, and set the brush to 90% hardness. I set the size to about 200.

I take a sample from the green area by *Ctrl-clicking* on it (1). Then I click once at the left, in the red area (2). As we can see, we made a *pure* clone, *Value* included (2). Now I select the *Heal* tool which is placed below the *Clone* tool in the toolbar. Its shortcut is *J*. Again I sample the green area by *Ctrl*-clicking on it,

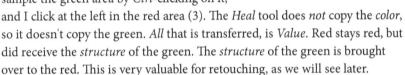

and I click at the left in the red area (3). The *Heal* tool does *not* copy the *color*, so it doesn't copy the green. *All* that is transferred, is *Value*. Red stays red, but did receive the *structure* of the green. The *structure* of the green is brought over to the red. This is very valuable for retouching, as we will see later.

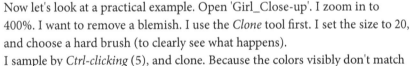

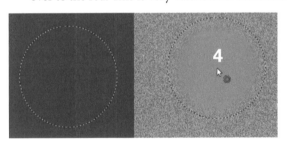

When I go the other way around, and copy *red* to *green*, we see the *structure* in the green is *removed* (4), because there isn't any structure in the red.

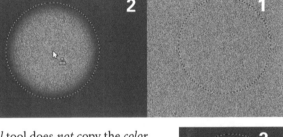

Now let's look at a practical example. Open 'Girl_Close-up'. I zoom in to 400%. I want to remove a blemish. I use the *Clone* tool first. I set the size to 20, and choose a hard brush (to clearly see what happens).

I sample by *Ctrl-clicking* (5), and clone. Because the colors visibly don't match (6), I *do not* want to clone *color*. Now let's repeat this with the *Heal* tool.

I press *Ctrl-Z*, and press *J* to select the *Heal* tool. I sample again by *Ctrl*-clicking (7), and click on the blemish (8). Now the color matches.

I open the *History* panel. By alternately pressing the *down* and *up* arrow key, I can *quickly* compare the before and after. We can see the *Heal* tool works well in situations with *color variations*.

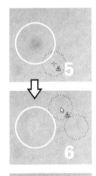

In the next lesson we will go a step further, and look at a professional skin retouching technique called Frequency Separation.

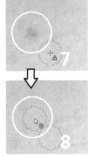

63. Professional skin retouching with frequency separation

In this lesson we will look at a professional skin improvement technique, called *Frequency separation*. With Frequency separation you can make skin look *smoother*, without losing the *texture* of the skin.

The way this is done, is by *splitting* the layer into two separate layers. One of these layers will *only* have the *Color* information, and the other layer will *only* have the *Value* information. And it is on the *Value* layer, where the skin *texture* will be visible. So if we smooth the skin by *blurring* the *Color* layer, we won't affect the skin *texture*. In the texture, or *Value* layer, we will *improve* the skin texture where needed, by removing texture *irregularities*, with the Heal or Clone tool.

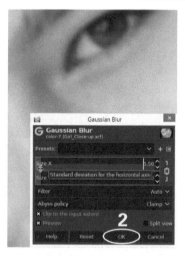

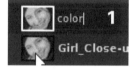

Open 'Girl_Close-up'. I start by duplicating the layer. I name the duplicate: Color (1). I will now *blur* the Color layer. As a result, we will *lose all* skin *texture*. The principle behind Frequency separation is, that the *detail* we lose by blurring, will be *transferred* to the Value layer. So from the Color layer, we're *pushing* the detail out, to the Value layer.

I go to: *Filters > Blur > Gaussian Blur*. So how *much* should I blur? A good rule of thumb is to blur just enough, until the *blemishes* have disappeared. If I blur more than that (which *isn't* needed), I will also start to push out *color* to the Value layer. And for a good separation, we want to *minimize color* in the Value layer. I will try 5.5. I click on *OK* (2). The Color layer is now ready.

Now let's create the Value layer. To do this, I set the Color layer to: *Grain extract* (3). What we are now seeing (4), will become the Value layer. To do this, I *right*-click on the Color layer, and choose: *New from Visible*. I call the layer: Value.

There is almost no color in the Value layer, which is good.

Now we have a (blurred) `Color` layer (5), and a (black and white) `Value` layer (6). On the `Color` layer is the color information, and in the `Value` layer is the texture information. I select the `Color` layer and set the blending mode *back* to *Normal*.

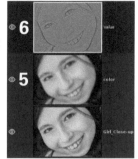

The last step is to make the `Color` and `Value` layer *work together* as if they were *one* layer. I set the `Value` layer to: *Grain merge*. Now the `Color` and `Value` layer act together as a single, 'normal' layer. By *Shift-clicking* on the original layer on the bottom, I can toggle between seeing the original layer, and the *frequency separated* layers. Visually, there is no difference. You could also place the Value and Color layer together in a layer *Group*.

Now let's start improving the skin. I start with the `Value` layer. I hide the original layer *and* the `Color` layer, so I can work on the `Value` layer. I will zoom in on the nose to 200%. I can see several light and dark skin *irregularities* in the skin texture, that I can remove. I press *J* to select the *Heal* tool. In the *Tool Options*, I select a hard brush, and set the size to 10. I will not remove the freckles now, but focus

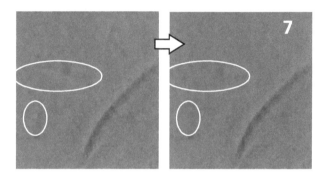

only on getting a smooth skin *texture*. I will remove the lighter and darker spots. As we can see, the skin texture has become less irregular and bumpy (7).

You could speed up this process by using *Heal selection* as we did before. It's a bit less precise, but you can work much faster. I press *Q* to enter *Quick mask mode*. At the bottom left I *right-click* on the Quick mask *icon*, and I *invert* the visibility of the mask by choosing: *Mask Selected Areas*. I use a hard brush at size 10. I zoom to 300%. I will click on some dark spots (8). I press *Q* again to get a selection. I go to: *Filters > Enhance > Heal Selection*. I will set *Context sampling* to 10 pixels, and click on *OK*. I press *Ctrl-D* to deselect. I have removed the dark spots. After making a new selection, I can *repeat* Heal Selection *immediately* by just pressing *Ctrl-F*. By pressing *Ctrl-F* you automatically *repeat the last filter*, with its *last used settings*.

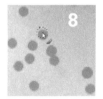

Now let's look at the `Color` layer. On the `Color` layer I will *smooth* the color of the skin in certain *areas*, to make the skin more even. A convenient way to work, is by using the *Free select* tool. With the *Free select* tool I will drag several *smaller* selections, like this one (9). After drawing a selection, I will *blur* the pixels inside that selection, on the `Color` layer.

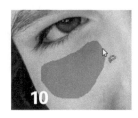

To prevent the blurring from being noticeable, it is important that the selection has a *soft edge*. I press Q. As we can see, right now the selection has a *hard* edge (10). I press Q to get a selection again. You can *smooth* the edge of a *selection* by going to: *Select > Feather*. I will try 40 pixels, and click on *OK*. I press Q to see the result (11). We can see now the selection has a soft edge. I press Q again.

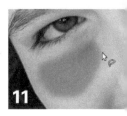

I can *also* set the feathering in the *Tool options*. I will activate *Feather edges*, and drag *Radius* to 40 (12). The *next* selection I draw, will *automatically* have a *feathered* edge (13). I can't *see* the feathered edge though (I can only see this in *Quick mask mode*). The 'marching ants' will 'walk' through the *middle* of the feathered edge. So I know that the *actual* size of my selection will be a bit *larger* than what the 'marching ants' show. Knowing this, I will avoid coming *to close* to the edges when I draw a selection, because I want to *avoid* mixing skin color, with other colors.

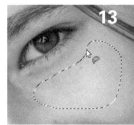

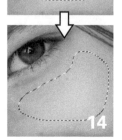

To *smooth* a selected piece of skin, I go to: *Filters > Blur > Gaussian Blur*. For the radius, I will try 30. When I click on *Preview*, I can see the color of the skin is getting smoother (14). I click on *OK*. Now I will repeat this. I draw a new selection. To quickly *reopen* Gaussian Blur, I can go to: Filters > *Re-Show Gaussian Blur*, or press *Shift-Ctrl-F*. The last used value, 30, is still active. I click *Cancel*. As we saw earlier, by pressing *Ctrl-F*, I can *repeat* the last used filter (using the last used values) *without* having to open the filter. So I *drag* a selection, press *Ctrl-F*, *drag* a selection again, press *Ctrl-F* again, and so on. Let's compare (15).

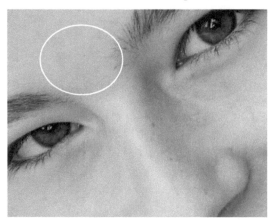

In the next lesson we will look at a powerful tool for retouching, called *Warp Transform*.

64. Warp Transform

Warp Transform is Gimp's variant of Photoshop's *Liquify*. It can be used for fun, like making someone's eyes really big, but when used subtly, like professional retouchers do, it becomes a serious retouching tool. I have opened 'Girl_close-up'. I will duplicate the layer. I select the *Warp Transform tool*, by going to: *Tools > Transform tools > Warp Transform* (1).

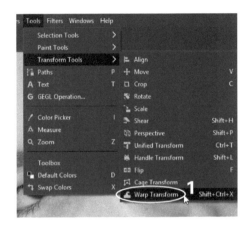

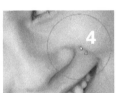

In the *Tool Options*, by default *Move pixels* is selected. If I click on it, I see I have six more brushes (2). Let's start with the *Move pixels* brush.

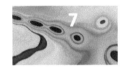

I will increase the *Size* to 400 (3).
When I drag, I see I am moving pixels (4). I press *Ctrl-Z* to undo. You can increase and decrease the *Hardness* of the brush (5). I think 50% works quite well. The higher you set the *Strength* of the brush (6), the less you *smear* pixels, and the more you *move* the pixels that are inside the brush.

When you move your mouse at normal speed, *Spacing* has no effect. But when you set spacing at 100 and move fast, you get special effects (7).
Let's try to make the nose thinner, by dragging the sides in (8). By pressing the eye of the top layer, I can compare the before and after. To apply the change(s) I made, I press *Enter* or select another tool. I duplicate the top layer again. With the *Grow area* brush you could make the eyes *larger*, and with the *Shrink area* brush, you could make the top of the nose *smaller*. *Swirl clockwise* and *counter-clockwise* can be used to give hair curvature (9). Before you apply the changes to a layer (by pressing *Enter* or selecting another tool), you're able to *undo* changes *locally* with the *Erase tool*.

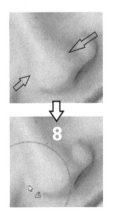

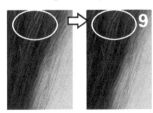

In the next lecture we'll look at dodging and burning.

65. Dodging and burning

Dodging and burning is the technique of selectively lightening and darkening an image. When you *dodge* an area, you make that area *lighter*, and when you *burn* an area, you make that area *darker*.

Dodging and burning is often used *after* Frequency separation, for example to accentuate the *contour* and *depth* of a face a bit more. We've already seen dodging and burning in action in lesson 30 about *layer mask uses*. In this lecture we will look at *another* method to dodge and burn.

Open 'Girl_Close-up'. For this method I create an empty layer *above* the layer I want to dodge and burn. I open the Color window. I click on the *HSV* icon (1) to get the HSV sliders. I drag *Value* to 50% to get a *middle grey* (2). I click on *OK*. I fill the empty layer with the grey, by pressing *Alt-Backspace* (3). I set the grey layer to *Overlay* (4), which will make the grey disappear like it's not there. I press *D* to set the Fore- and Background color to black and white. I press *B* to select the brush, and in the *Tool Options* I select a brush with 0% hardness. I set the size to about 250. I set the brush *Opacity* to about 10%. I now paint in the grey layer.

With *black* I can *burn*, and accentuate the shadows. When I want to *dodge*, I simply press *X* to *switch* the Fore- and Background color to *white*.

There are *two advantages* of this method over the *mask* method described in lesson 30. First, there is *no pre-set limit* to the *depth* of the dodging and burning. And second, you *don't* have to *switch layers*, because you're working on just *one* layer.

In the next chapter we will look at how to make a book cover.

Chapter 7

Making e-book covers

66. Make a basic e-book cover

In this lecture we'll make an e-book cover. So what *size* should an e-book cover be? When we look on the Amazon Kindle website, we see that the average e-book cover has an *aspect ratio* of 1.5. This means that the height is 50% larger than the width. And a popular size for self-published books is 6 by 9 inches, which *also* has an aspect ratio of 1.5. So this matches.

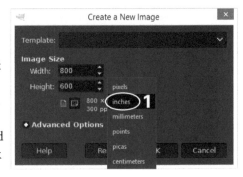

Now that we now the aspect ratio, how many *pixels* should our e-book cover be? Amazon recommends for an e-book cover a *minimum height* of 2500 pixels. Let's also have a look at the pixel dimensions of a 6 by 9 inches file, at 300 dpi (which is needed for a printed book). I go to: *File > New*. I click on *pixels (px)*, and choose: *inches* (1). For *Width* I fill in 6, and for *Height* I fill in 9 (2). I open *Advanced Options*, and set *pixels/in* (**p**ixels **p**er **i**nch, short: ppi, or *dpi*) to 300 (3). We see this will give us a file of 1800 x 2700 pixels (4). 2700 pixels is only *slightly* larger than Amazon's minimum requirement of 2500 pixels height. The *advantage* of 2700 pixels is that it now meets the requirements for *both* an e-book cover, *and* a 6 by 9 inch book cover for *print*. I click on *OK*.

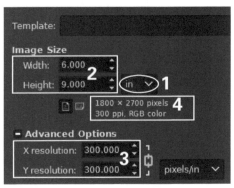

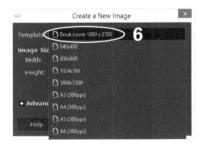

Let's *save* this document as a *template* for reusing. I go to: *File > Create Template* (5). I will name it: *book cover 1800x2700*, and click on *OK*. Now I go to: *File > New*, and at the top I click on *Template*. Here I see my e-book cover template (6). I select it, and click on *OK*.

Now let's open an image that we will use for the cover. Open 'Skyline'. The image comes from a website called *Unsplash.com*. Unsplash offers free, high quality images that come with a *Creative Commons Zero* license. This means: *'you can copy, modify, distribute and use the photos for free, including commercial purposes, without asking permission from or providing attribution to the photographer or Unsplash'*.

I drag the image over to my template. I place the image so I see

the water and the buildings (6). Now I will place some *guides*, that will help me with placing my text. To do this, I press *Ctrl-A* to get a selection around my document.

Then I go to: *Select > Shrink*. I type 250 (7), and press Enter (8). Now I go to: *Image > Guides > New Guides from selection*. I press *Ctrl-D* to deselect (9).

If I want to *hide* the guides, I go to: View > *Show Guides*, or press *Ctrl-;*. I can *move* guides with the *Move* tool while holding the *Shift* key down. When I press *Shift* and come close to a guide, the guide will turn red. Then I can move the guide. To *remove* a guide, I simply drag the guide *off* the image. To undo a guide change, press *Ctrl-Z*. To *add* guides by hand, I go to *View > Show Rulers*. Out of the Rulers at the left and the top, I can now *drag* guides (10).

The fonts I will use are: *League Gothic* and *Montserrat*. I downloaded them from *fontsquirrel.com* (11). This is a website for free and professional looking fonts, that can be used *commercially*. The fonts have a *SIL Open Font License*. This means that the fonts can be used commercially and can even be redistributed, as long as they are not being sold. Click on: *Download OTF*. OTF stands for: *Open Type Font*. I open the downloaded *League Gothic* folder. League Gothic has *four* font weights (12). You install a font by *double*-clicking on it. Then click on the *Install* button.

To get good contrast for my title, I will use dark text because I have a light background. I select the color picker, and sample a dark blue from a building (13).

My title will be: *Summer in the city*. I will make the word city large. I click on the text tool, and drag a frame on the canvas. Because the guides are *magnetic*, I can now drag the sides of the text frame *against* the guides, and they will *snap* like a magnet (14).

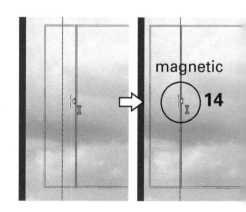

In the *Tool Options* I select the text below *Font* (15), and type: le (16). From the menu that I get, I select *League Gothic* (17). I press *Caps Lock* to type with capitals. I click inside the text frame and type CITY. In the *Tool Options*, behind *Justify*, I click on the *Centered* icon. Then, behind *Size*, I click in the text entry field. I press the arrow up key and hold it

down until the text fits the frame (18). If the text frame isn't *high* enough, I'll drag bottom of the frame down (19). When I press *Alt*, I can drag the text frame. Let's experiment with the space *between* the letters a bit. To be able to experiment, I'll create a bit more space by dragging the *sides* of the text frame to the *document edges*, where they will *also* snap.

Under *Justify*, I click in the *Adjust letter spacing* text entry field. With the arrow up key I increase the letter spacing to about 32 (20).

Now I will *duplicate* the text layer. In the *Tool Options*, behind *Size*, I click in the text entry field and press the down arrow key to make the text smaller (to 200). I press the *Alt* key, and drag the text frame up until it snaps against the *upper* guide. I select the text and type: A SUMMER. In the *Tool Options* I select the text under Font, and type: mo. From the menu I select *Montserrat Bold*. I will adjust the size of the text so it doesn't go *outside* the guides. I drag the bottom of the text frame *up*, so the two text frames I now have *don't overlap* (21).

I duplicate the text layer again. I press *Alt*, and drag the text frame between A SUMMER and CITY. I select the text, and type: IN THE. In the *Tool Options* I click in the text entry field, and with the down arrow key I set the size to about 100. I drag the bottom of the text field up again to avoid overlap. At the top, the text is ready (22).

Next I will create a *line*. I create a new layer by *Shift-clicking* on the new layer button. I press *M* to select the *Rectangle* select tool. I drag a selection *across* the complete *width* of the canvas. In the *Tool Options* under *Size*, I will set the *height* of my selection to 5 pixels (23). The width of the selection is 1800 pixels, which is the width of my document. Now I have a *selection* of 1800 by 5 pixels, which will become my line (24).

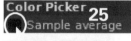

To pick a color for the line, I zoom in close on an orange area. I select the *Color Picker* tool. To be able to take the color of a *single pixel*, I *deselect* *Sample average* in the *Tool Options* (25). I click on an orange pixel (26). I open the Color window, and adjust the orange a bit. Now I press *Alt-Backspace* to fill the selection. I press *Ctrl-D* to deselect.

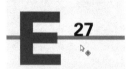

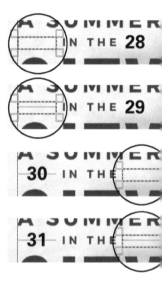

I press *V* to select the *Move* tool, and drag the red line to about the middle of the text IN THE. I zoom in to 200% on the letter E. With my up and down arrow keys, I can nudge the line perfectly to the middle of the E (27). I don't want to see the line everywhere. So I will *hide* the line with a *mask*, and *reveal* the parts I want to see. I *right-click* on the line layer, and choose *Add Layer Mask*. I select *Black*, and press *Enter*. To reveal the line, I press *M* to select the *Rectangle* select tool. I will drag a selection at the left of the text IN (28). The selection will *snap* to the left guide. I press *D* to set the Fore- and Background colors to their default. I press *Ctrl-Backspace* to fill the selection with *white* (29). Now I *drag* the selection to the right side, where it will snap against the right ruler (30). I fill with white again to reveal the line at the right side (31). I press *Ctrl-D* to deselect.

At the bottom I will place the author's name. I duplicate the IN THE text layer, and drag it to the bottom. To change the color of the text, in the *Tool Options* I click on the *Color thumbnail* (32). I select white and click on *OK*. I select the text and type the author's name: Mark Spring. Under *Justify*, I click in the *Adjust letter spacing* text entry field. With the arrow up key I will increase the letter spacing a bit more. I press *Ctrl-;* to hide the guides. Our book cover is finished (33)!

So how will the e-book cover look like on Amazon's website? Before I make a smaller version of the book cover, I will first *save* the document, so I don't lose any work by accident. I go to: *File > Save as*. I name my file: *City-book-cover*.

Now I go to: *Image > Duplicate*. With de *duplicate* I can experiment with the image, without affecting the original. I will start by turning my document into a *single layer*. To do this, I *right-click* in the layers panel, and choose at the bottom: *Flatten Image* (34). All layers have now been merged into *one* layer.

So at what size are the book cover thumbnails shown on Amazon? At this moment, most thumbnails on Amazon are 160 pixels high. To rescale my image to the Amazon thumbnail size, I go to: *Image > Scale Image.* I select the text behind *Height*, type 160, and click on *Scale* (35). I press *Ctrl-1* to see the thumbnail at 100%. Now let's place our thumbnail in the actual Amazon Kindle store web page.

I will make a screenshot of the Amazon Kindle store web page. I do this by pressing the *Print Screen* key on my keyboard. If I don't want to capture the entire screen, but only the *active window*, I hold down the *Alt* key while pressing the *Print Screen* key. In Gimp, I go to: *File > Create > From Clipboard* (36). I press *Ctrl-1* to get a 100% view. I drag the City thumbnail over to the screenshot file, and drag it over another thumbnail, to see the result (37). With my arrow keys, I can move the thumbnail *one pixel* at a time for exact placing.

When you're working on the cover, and you want to have a *preview* of the cover *at thumbnail size* (for example to check the *readability* of the text), you can quickly zoom out, by *Ctrl*-scrolling to *6,25%*, shown at the bottom of the screen (38). The image will then be *168 pixels high*, only a few pixels larger than the Amazon thumbnail size.

In the next lesson we will make a more advanced book cover, where the focus will be on using blending modes.

New York Times Best Sellers

37

A SUMMER
— IN THE —

CITY

MARK SPRING

‹

★★★★⯨ 4,922
List price: $27.99

67. Make an e-book cover using blending modes

For our second book cover the focus will be on the use of blending modes. For our cover I will use two grunge textures. An easy way to find images that can be used *commercially* is to use Google images. I will search for: `grunge`

Grunge Texture Png

`texture`. When I click on *Search tools* at the right, I get several extra options. I click on: *Usage rights* (1), and choose: *labelled for commercial reuse with modification* (2). Just to be safe, I will also click on the image to visit the website,

so I can double-check that the image is really 'free' to use. One of the grunge

textures comes from *indiedesigner.com* (3), and one comes from *Aqueoussun* (4). On both sites I can find the *Terms of use*.

Open 'kensal_green'. I will use this image to give *text* a grunge effect. To

prepare the image for this, I go to: *Colors > Threshold*. This tool will make pixels *either* pure black, *or* pure white. By moving the black slider (5) to the left more pixels get white, and by moving it to the right more pixels get black. I drag a bit to the right. I click on *OK*. I press *T* to select the *Text* tool, and click on the canvas. I type in capitals: `DEER`. In the *Tool Options* I select the text below *Font*, and type: `le`. From the menu I select *League Gothic*. In the text *Size* entry field I set the size to 1000 and press *Enter*. To be able to experiment with the 'look' we are going to get, I will use a blending mode. I *Shift-click* on the create a new layer icon. I

drag the new layer on the bottom, and fill it with white (6) by pressing *Ctrl-Backspace*. I drag the *text* layer between the other layers. I select the grunge layer on top (7), and set it's blending mode to *Lighten only*. Now we can see the grunge effect we will get inside the text (8).

I press *V* to select the *Move* tool and select the text layer. I will drag the text to different places, to see different results. I can also move the text by holding down *Shift* and using the *arrow* keys, which goes fast. And I could experiment with bigger and smaller text to get different results. When I'm ready, I select the grunge layer. I *Alt*-click on the *text* layer to get its selection. Then I press *Ctrl-J* to make a new layer from the selection (9). I set the *blending mode* of the *Ctrl-J* layer *back* to *Normal*.

Now I open the e-book *template*. I go to: *File > New*. From the Template menu I choose the *e-book template* we made in the last lecture. I press *Ctrl-A* to get a selection around the document. Then I go to: *Select > Shrink*. I type 250, and press Enter. I go to: *Image > Guides > New Guides from selection*. I press *Ctrl-D* to deselect.

I go to my grunge document. I *only* need the *top* layer, so I drag the *top* layer over. The background image I am going to use comes from *Unsplash.com*. I open 'Deer'. The deer image is much *smaller* than the book cover template; it is only *1025* pixels high. To fill the template, it will have to be *2700* pixels high. Because the image doesn't have much detail, it will be no problem to enlarge it. I go to: *Image > Scale Image*. I set *Height* to 2700 pixels, and click on *Scale* (10).

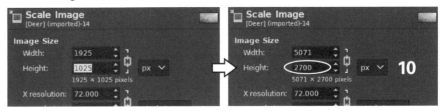

Now that the deer image has the correct height, I drag it over to the template. I will drag the watching deer in the middle (11).

I will now *intensify* the light and the colors of the image with a blending mode from the lighten group; *Dodge*. I create a new layer, and call it Dodge. With the *Color picker* I click on the deer. I fill the Dodge layer with the brown color sampled from the deer by pressing *Alt-Backspace*. I set the layer's blending mode to *Dodge*. The result will be quite bright. To change this, I press *Ctrl-L* to open *Levels*. I drag the midtone slider to the right to darken the result. Now the image has a nice warm *glowing orange*. I also would like to shift the color of the image a bit more to yellow. To do this, I press *Ctrl-U* to open *Hue-Saturation*. To move from Red more to Yellow, I drag *Hue* to the right.

Now I will add a grungy effect to the image. I open 'Metal_Paint'. I drag the image over. I will *rotate* the Metal_Paint layer. I go to: *Layer > Transform > Rotate 90° clockwise*. I drag the Metal_Paint layer *below* the *Dodge* layer, and set it to *Overlay*. I lower the *Opacity* to about 70% (12).

Now let's include the text. I drag the DEER text layer we made before, on top. I will color the black text brown. I go to *Colors > Colorize*. To be able to colorize *black* pixels, you first have to *increase Lightness* a bit (13). Now I drag the *Hue* slider to a brown (14). To lose the *white* pixels in the text (15), I will set the layer to *Multiply* (16).

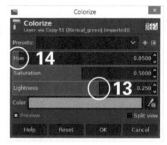

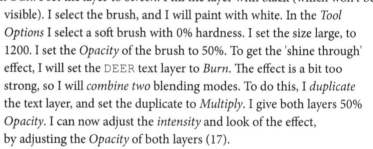

I would like to have a *light source* shining *through* the text. Below the *Dodge* layer, I create a new layer.

I call it Sun. I set the layer to *Screen*. I fill the layer with black (which won't be visible). I select the brush, and I will paint with white. In the *Tool Options* I select a soft brush with 0% hardness. I set the size large, to 1200. I set the *Opacity* of the brush to 50%. To get the 'shine through' effect, I will set the DEER text layer to *Burn*. The effect is a bit too strong, so I will *combine two* blending modes. To do this, I *duplicate* the text layer, and set the duplicate to *Multiply*. I give both layers 50% Opacity. I can now adjust the *intensity* and look of the effect, by adjusting the *Opacity* of both layers (17).

I will also *link* the two text layers so they will move as *one*.

I open the *City* book cover we made in the previous lesson. I drag the IN THE text layer over so I can use it again. I place it on top. I select the text, and type: THE SECRET OF THE (18).
I select the *Move* tool, and click on the canvas once. Now with the arrow keys, I will position the text. I will align the start of the H, with the start of the D (19).

I duplicate the text layer and type the author's name: MARK SPRING.
To set the color I click in the *Tool Options* on the
color thumbnail and choose black. Black is a bit dark,
so I lower the *Opacity* of the text *layer* to get a lighter
tint. With the *Color picker* I now *sample* the color of
the text (20). Then I set the *Opacity* of the text layer
back to 100%. I *double-click* on the text layer. In the
Tool Options I click on the color thumbnail again.

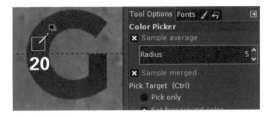

I select the *eyedropper* from the *Text Color window*, and now click on
the *Foreground color*; on the color I just sampled (21).

The reason that I originally used the *Color picker* from the *toolbar*, is that
I can use the *Sample average* option in the *Tool Options* (sample an *average*
of several pixels). The eyedropper from the *Text Color window*, and the
eyedropper from the *Change Foreground Color window*, both don't have
this option and will sample a *single* pixel.

In the next lesson we will finish our e-book cover using
blending modes.

68. Finish an e-book cover using blending modes

Let's do some last adjustments. I would like to lighten up the shadows at the bottom a bit. I duplicate the *Dodge* layer, that I used to lighten up the colors of the deer image. I *right-click* on the duplicate, and choose: *Add Layer Mask*. I select *Black*, and press *Enter*. I set the blending mode to *Screen*. I select a soft brush, and set its size to 300. I set the *Opacity* of the brush to 50%. Because the brush will *also* be magnetic, I go to *View* and uncheck both *Snap to guides*, and *Snap to Canvas Edges* for a moment (1). Now I paint with white over the shadows. Because the result looks a bit greenish, I select the *content thumbnail* of the layer, and open *Hue-Saturation*.

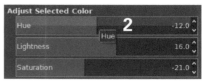

To move from green to yellow and red, I drag the *Hue* slider to the left (2). I will also increase the *lightness* a bit, and *desaturate*.

To make the authors name stand out more, I will put a lighter box behind the name. I create a new layer below the text layer. I press *M* to select the *Rectangle*

select tool, and drag a box around the text. I zoom in a bit and adjust the selection. I could round the corners, but I will leave the corners sharp. I fill the selection with white, and deselect. I lower the *Opacity* of the layer to 10%. I select the *Move* tool, and click on the canvas. With my arrow keys, I can fine-tune the placement of the box (3).

I also would like to give the text on top a bit glow. I create a new layer *below* the text layer. I *Alt-click* on the text layer to get its selection, and press *Alt-Backspace* to fill with white. I deselect. I go to: *Filters > Blur > Gaussian Blur*. I set the *Blur Size* to about 5 (4), and click on *OK*. I set the blending mode of the layer to *Overlay*.

To make the glow stronger, I *duplicate* the glow layer (5). I can adjust the *strength* of the glow, by adjusting the *Opacity* of the layer.

Finally, I would like to have some leaves at the top. Below the *Dodge* layers, I create a new layer and call it `leaves`. I set its blend mode to *Multiply*. I select the brush. In the *Tool Options* I click on the brush icon, and click on the *View as list* icon (6). I drag the scrollbar to the bottom and select *Texture Hose 01*. I set the size to 400, and the *Opacity* to 20%. With black, I paint around the text close to the edge (7).

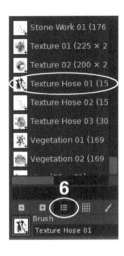

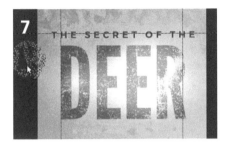

I will also manually add a bit of a vignette effect, making the *edges* a bit *darker* than the inside of the document. Below the *Dodge* layers, I create a new layer, and set the blend mode to *Multiply*. I select a soft brush, size 700. I set the brush *Opacity* quite low, to 5%. Now I will darken the right edge a bit (8). Our e-book cover is finished!

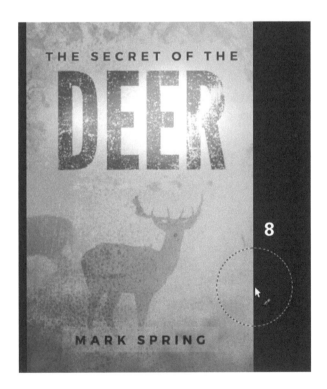

Chapter 8

Adjusting Gimp's User Interface

69. Configuring Gimp's User Interface

In this lecture we will look at how to change Gimp's User interface. To add a panel to a panel group, click on: *Configure this tab*, go to: *Add Tab*, and choose the panel you want to add (1).

To remove a panel from a panel group, click on its tab, click on: *Configure this tab*, and choose: *Close tab* (2).

You can have a panel displayed with text, with an icon, or both. Click on: *Configure this tab*, click on: *Tab Style*, and choose an option (3).

You can change the order of the tabs, by dragging a tab to another position (4). You can also drag a panel to another panel group.

You can have a have a *floating* panel, by dragging a panel out of a group (5). You can place a floating panel where you want.

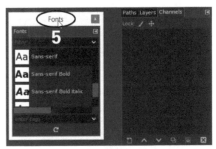

You can also create a new panel *column*. If you drag a panel to the left side, you will see a line and an arrow appearing (6). Then release the mouse (7).

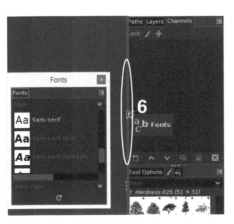
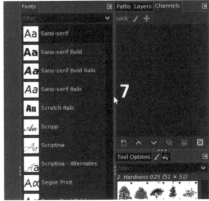

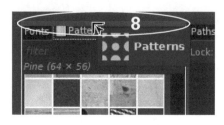

I can *add* tabs again. To create a *new* panel *row*, drag a panel to the top (8). When you see a *line* and an *arrow* appearing, release the mouse. You can adjust the size of the panel *columns*, and panel *rows* (9).

You can also place panels at the left side of the UI, for example the *Tool Options* (10). When you have created a workspace that you like, you can *save* the workspace. Go to: *Edit > Preferences*. Click on the *Window Management* tab, and click on: *Save Window Positions Now*. From now on, when you open up Gimp, this will be

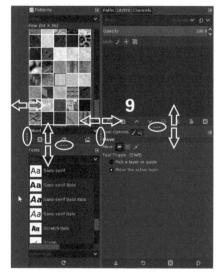

your default workspace. I click on *Cancel*. If you want a certain *tool* to behave different (by default), you

can *also* save those changes. If you want for example the *Color Picker* to have a higher *Sample average Radius* by default, for example 10 (11), or if you want a different *default brush* when you open Gimp and select the *Paintbrush*, you can make these changes permanent, by going to: *Edit > Preferences*.

Click on the *Tool Options* tab, and click on: *Save Tool Options Now*. Saving tool behaviour is best done directly after opening Gimp, because all other Tool Option changes made since you opened Gimp, will then also be saved.

New in Gimp 2.10.**18** is the possibility to *group* tools. Using 'tool groups' means some tools will be *hidden* in your Toolbar. To reveal a hidden tool, you have to click and hold your mouse down on a tool that has a little *arrow* (12). The little arrow means there are one or more hidden tools behind that tool. You can then select from a small *drop-down menu* a different tool from that 'tool group'. I don't have 'tool grouping' activated (I just show how it looks at the left). To *activate* 'tool groups', go to: *Edit > Preferences*. Click on the *Toolbox* tab. Below *'Tools Configuration'*, you can see the tools are presented in the same order as they appear in your *Toolbar*. An *eye* at the left of a tool means that tool is visible in your *Toolbar*. To hide a tool, click on the eye in front of that tool. The eye (and the corresponding tool in your *Toolbar*) will disappear. Click there again and the eye (and tool) are visible again. Your *Toolbar* will directly update any changes you make in the *Preferences*! If you want a tool at a higher or lower location in your *Toolbar*, you can simply *drag* that tool in the *Preferences* to another place.

Because I haven't *'Use tool groups'* activated, the folders that you see (all named *'Group'*) don't have a function yet. When I now click on *'Use tool groups'* (13) a little cross in front of the text shows it is activated. As soon as I activated *'Use tool groups'*, several tools disappeared from my *Toolbar*. This is because now the *'Group'* folders have become *activated*. And from each *'Group'* folder, only **one** tool will be shown in your *Toolbar*; namely the *highest placed* visible tool that is in a folder. Tools that are below the highest placed tool in a Group will now be *hidden* in your *Toolbar*. Note: Tools that don't have an eye checked will *never* be shown. Every tool that you want to be revealed in your *Toolbar* needs its eye to be checked. You can *move tools* to another place. You can look at the situation we have now as a normal folder structure. This means you can drag a tool to another location *within* a folder, but you're also allowed to place a tool *outside* a folder (tools don't *have* to be inside a folder). A tool that is placed on its own (so isn't inside a folder) *won't* have a little arrow in the *Toolbar* (because it is not hiding other tools). You can drag a tool from *one* folder to *another* folder. Groups as a whole can also be moved up or down in the

stacking order. If you prefer not to drag, you can also move Groups (and tools) with the *up* and *down arrows* (14). Placing a tool in another Group however, and placing a tool outside a Group, needs dragging. You can create a new Group by clicking on the *'Create a new tool group'* icon (15). And by clicking on the *eye* of a Group, you hide the whole Group (its content included). And lastly: you're also able to click on a tool in the *Toolbar*. This tool will then become *selected* in the *Preferences* window!

Right now, we have Gimp's *dark* theme. To choose another theme, go on the *Theme* tab. You can have a Gray theme, a Light theme, and Gimp's Default theme. *Independent* from the Theme, under *Icon Theme*, you can choose an icon set, like *Color* and *Legacy*. *Symbolic-Inverted* (16) works best with Gimp's lighter themes.

You can make the icons smaller, or larger (17). The larger icons will be better visible on *High Resolution Displays*.

If you want *another language* for the program, go to the *Interface* tab (18). At the top you can choose a language from the list. After restarting Gimp, the language will be changed. To save the changes and exit the *Preferences*, click on *OK*.

Chapter 9

Gimp specifics

70. Focus in GIMP

In this book I have tried to take away the differences between Gimp and Photoshop. The differences that remain are described in this chapter. I will explain why these differences are there, and how to deal with them.

A difference between Gimp and Photoshop is *focus*. If I click on the *Layers* panel, I can walk through the layers with my up and down arrow keys, to select a different layer (1, 2). I can however *also* use the arrow keys to *move* the content of a layer, as we have done before. To be able to do this, I first clicked on the canvas. By clicking on the canvas, I take the focus away from the layers panel, and *bring* the focus to the canvas. Now the arrow keys behave in a different way; they can now be used to *move* the content of the selected layer.

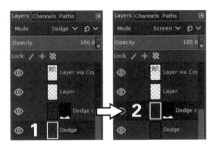

In Photoshop you *can't* walk through the layers with the arrow keys. Instead, in Photoshop you will *always* move the content on the canvas. If you prefer not to *left-click* on the canvas, because of the possibility of moving something, you can *double-right-click* on the canvas instead. *Right-clicking* will *only* show a *menu*, and right-clicking again will *hide* the menu again. So *double-right-clicking* is a quick and *safe way* to bring focus to the canvas for using the *arrow keys*.

In the next lesson we will look at the active tool.

71. The active tool

If you *click* on the canvas and a color adjustment opens, for example *Levels*, the reason for this happening is that Levels was the *last used tool*. Let's have a look.

I press *Ctrl-L* to do a *Levels* adjustment, and click *OK*. Although the Levels *window* has now closed, Levels is *still* the *selected tool*, which we also can see in the *Tool options* (1). So if I click on the canvas, Levels *re-opens* again. Unlike in Photoshop, in Gimp the color adjustments are *also* tools, and can be added in the *toolbox* if you want to. *Like* in Photoshop, a tool *will stay active* until you choose *another* tool.

So when a color adjustment opens after clicking on the canvas, just click on the tool you *intended* to use, for example the *Move* tool, and the color adjustment window will close *automatically*.

In the next lesson we will look at the Floating selection.

72. The floating selection

In Gimp we have the 'Photoshop way' of pasting pixels. If I press *Ctrl-C* and *Ctrl-V*, I will get a *new* layer with the copied content. This is the same behaviour as in Photoshop. However, it is not the *default* way of pasting in Gimp. If we go to: *Edit > Paste as*, we can see in the submenu that *Ctrl-V* has been assigned to *New Layer* (1). It is *not* assigned to the *Paste* command in the main menu (2).

Let's click on the *Paste* command and see what happens.

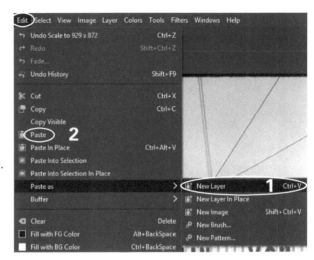

What we now see is a *Floating Selection (Layer 1 copy)* layer (3). By clicking on the *Create a new layer icon* (4), I turn it into a *normal* layer (*Layer 1 copy*) (5).
I press *Ctrl-Z* to undo. If I click on the *Anchor the floating layer* icon (6), the Floating Selection layer will be *merged down* to the layer below (7).

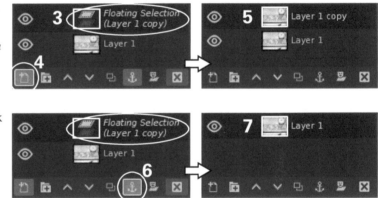

A *Floating Selection* is Gimp's version of Photoshop's *Ctrl-J*. Let's have a look at how *Ctrl-J* is done *without* the *Layer-via-copy* plugin.
I make a selection with the *Rectangle* select tool. I press *Ctrl-C* to copy the pixels *inside* the selection. I go to: *Edit > Paste*. Then I click on the Create a new layer icon. We now have the same result as pressing *Ctrl-J*.
The *difference* is, that with *Ctrl-J* we need *two steps less* to get the same result.

In the next lesson we will look at the Layer Boundary.

73. The layer boundary

In Gimp a layer has a boundary, called the layer Boundary. By default, the layer Boundary has the same size as the image itself. When I make the content of a layer smaller (1), the layer Boundary has shrunken, *together* with the layer content.

If I want to paint or clone on this layer (which I normally wouldn't do; I would use a *new layer* for this to work non-destructively), I see I cannot paint or work *outside* the layer Boundary (2).

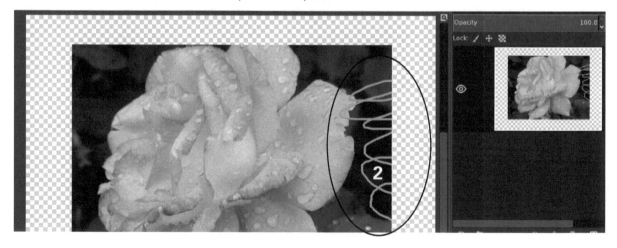

I can set the layer Boundary *back* to the image size, by going to: *Layer > Layer to Image Size* (3).

Now I can paint on the whole layer (4).

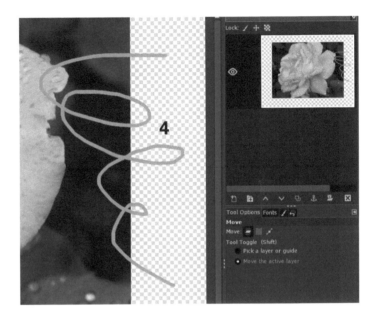

INDEX

Printed in Poland
by Amazon Fulfillment
Poland Sp. z o.o., Wrocław

33

31597767R10134